My Favourite Recipes

The publishers wish to thank Methodist Girls' School and
Dr Eileen Aw for the loan of crockery, kitchenware and a
tablecloth used by Mrs Ellice Handy and the school, and
Books Actually for the loan of vintage glaasware.

First published in 1952 and reprinted in 1954. Revised
editions in 1960, 1971, 1972, 1974 and reprinted twice in
1975, and reprinted again in 1976. Further revised editions in
1980 and 1990. This edition, 2012.

Food preparation for photography:
Anita Fam, Dulcie Ng, TA Tybally, Vivian Valledor Velu

Published by
Landmark Books Pte Ltd
5001 Beach Road
#02-73/74
Singapore 199588

Landmark Books is an imprint of Landmark Books Pte Ltd

ISBN 978-981-4189-39-2

Printed by Craft Print International Limited

My Favourite Recipes

Ellice Handy

◇LANDM△RK◇BOOKS◇

Table of Contents

My
Favourite
Recipes

Ellice Handy

Foreword

to the first edtion

In this book are a few recipes, not for those who know everything about cooking, but for those who have a desire to learn to cook. In the years I have been interested in cooking, I have made my own collection of recipes, ideas for which were suggested by friends or borrowed from cookery books. In these pages are some recipes from my collection.

As imagination must go into the making of every dish, I ask all who buy this book to use their imagination and make changes to my recipes, especially of local dishes, to suit their taste. You may prefer more of one ingredient and less of another. No two people cook the same dish the same way, and yet both can produce equally good results. The only way to develop a good hand at cooking is to practise in your kichen. In time, you will be able to cook your favourite dishes without using a recipe book.

Ellice Handy
1952

Facing: The first edition with the cover design by Mrs Tan Yoong Thye and Shirley Lim.

Introduction

by Sim Ee Waun

Ellice Handy is to Singapore, what Julia Child and Elizabeth David are to the United States. A foodie through and through, Mrs Handy was a culinary pioneer. During a time when society was less affluent, when travel was confined to an exclusive elite, imported goods were few and most Singaporeans were largely limited to eating their own native cuisine, she showed Singaporeans how to eat well, have an adventurous palate and explore other cuisines and cooking. A modern woman for her time, she was the first Singaporean to publish a cookbook – *My Favourite Recipes* in 1952. Not only is it the culinary classic on Singapore food, it is also a cornerstone of Singapore's culinary history today, for within its pages lie the culinary heritage of a nation.

Mrs Handy was also very much a product of her time, and expounded the need for economy and resourcefulness in the home kitchen – a virtue expected of any good housewife then. She was also a foodie during a period when there was little talk about cholesterol, sugar intake and weight loss… but it was also a more gracious period when daily life was dotted with afternoon teas on the verandah, homemade fruit cake and coconut candy. Her recipes all reflect her time.

Born Ellice Zuberbuhler in 1902, Ellice Handy spent her entire life associated with Methodist Girls' School – first as a student and boarder from the age of four at its boarding house, Nind Home, at 11 Mt Sophia, then as a teacher from 1922 and finally as the school's first Singaporean principal in 1948-1952 where she was tasked with rebuilding the school after the ravages of World War II. During this last period, she also visited the female prisoners on death row to see to their needs and offer comfort. For her work with MGS, she was given the OBE in 1950. In 1952, she compiled *My Favourite Recipes* and donated the proceeds to the school's building fund.

Her first encounter with food preparation was watching Miss Sophia Blackmore, the school's founder, prepare some leftover chicken and ham on a chafing dish with white sauce. Miss Blackmore later sent her to learn cooking in order to prepare lunch for the teachers. Mrs Handy recounted: "I was perhaps only 13 then, but under the supervision of Madam Lee Ling Neo, the matron of the Chinese and Indian girls in the school, I learnt to make my first curries and prepare the sambal tray." This sparked off a life-long passion for cooking.

An avid home cook, she collected recipes from friends whenever she encountered a dish she enjoyed and would adjust it here and there to suit her family's taste. "She loved cooking and being in the kitchen. It satisfied her creativity," said her daughter, Mrs Helen Angerson-Handy. "She had a flair for cooking. Even without a recipe, she was able to taste a dish and work out the ingredients that went into it. She had a good sense of taste, smell and she had good hands – small dainty hands… she had a light touch with her hands." She also loved entertaining at home – the more the merrier – and her large kitchen table was constantly a focal point of activity. Friends who came round would converge at the table to watch her cook, and when it was a quiet day at home, her daughters would do their schoolwork there while watching their mother busy herself in the kitchen with the help of the maid, Ah Foon.

Her favourite dishes appeared often during luncheons at home whether with or without guests – mee siam, popiah – including skins she made herself – kueh pie tie, rojak, curries, pineapple tarts and cakes for tea. In the evenings, she would cook western dishes as her husband, an Englishman, liked his traditional roasts, meatloaf and baked chicken for dinner. After she retired, Mrs Handy continued to tutor a handful of students in English, and it was after these tuition sessions that she would whip out homemade butter and ginger cakes and tea as treats. These she would serve on fine china tea sets which she loved. Mrs Handy also always had cake for her morning tea and, according to Helen, "very nice sandwiches."

Everyone remembers her coconut candy. "Whenever there was the church bazaar, she would make her coconut candy. She would get four or five friends round to help and they would make it over a hot charcoal stove," remembers her adopted daughter Mrs Jean Tow. Made with vanilla and chocolate flavouring, or coloured pink with cochineal, they were always sold out very quickly.

Of her kitchen, Jean remembers it to be spick and span, but with Mrs Handy's distinct touch. "You should have seen her kitchen," says Jean. "It was full of pots and pans, ingredients for baking cakes and such. She used to say, 'Whenever I want to cook something or bake a cake, I want to have the ingredients available.'"

For Mrs Handy, perhaps a traditionalist at heart, cooking was ultimately for the family. Adjusting recipes to suit one's palate was necessary, and expounded the need for practice. "There are no born cooks," said Mrs Handy in earlier writings. "Many have become good cooks from actually trying out recipes in their own kitchens…. Cooking is fun and should be enjoyed, not regarded as a chore.

"To become good at cooking, all you need is a love of tasty wholesome food, an observant eye, practice and imagination."

Mrs Handy cooked into her old age and at 85, moved to Australia to live with Helen. Even when her eyesight failed, Mrs Handy continued cooking, and her heart remained in Singapore until she died of a stroke two and half years later.

Sim Ee Waun is a freelance food writer and an aluma of Methodist Girls' School.

Weights and Measures

This edition includes the original weights and measures given by Mrs Handy in Malayan and imperial units. Conversions in metric units, rounded up, are also given. The precise conversions are given below.

Note that Mrs Handy used evaporated and condensed milk as fresh milk was not readily available when she wrote the recipes. For the same reason, she made her own buttermilk by adding lime juice to evaporated milk.

MEASUREMENTS AND CONVERSIONS
(All measurements level)

1 tahil ... 1 oz ... 37.8 g
1 kati ... 16 tahils ... 1⅓ lbs ... 605 g

1 cup liquid ... 8 fl oz ... ½ pint
1 cup flour (sifted) ... 4 oz ... 113.4 g
1 cup sugar ... 8 oz ... 226.8 g
1 cup butter ... 8 oz ... 226.8 g

Some measuring cups give 10 oz (283.5 g) to a cup, while others give 8 oz (226.8 g). The recipes in this book use the 8 oz (226.8 g) cup.

OVEN TEMPERATURES

Slow oven
250 - 325°F (121 - 163°C)
Casseroles, Rich Fruit Cake, Milk Puddings, Slow Roasting, Custards, Fish, Butter Cakes.

Moderate oven
350 - 400°F (177 - 204°C)
Sponges, Roast Meat.

Moderately hot oven
375 - 450°F (191 - 232°C)
Bread, Layer Cakes, Small Cakes, Buns.

Hot oven
450 - 475°F (232 - 246°C)
Pastry – Choux and Short.

Very hot oven
475 - 500°F (246 - 260°C)
Pastry – Flaky and Puff, Scones.

Gas Oven
Regulo 1   250°F (121°C)
Regulo 4   350°F (177°C)
Regulo 6-7 400°F (204°C)
Regulo 8   450°F (323°C)
Regulo 10 500°F (260 °C)

General Tips

HOW TO MAKE COCONUT MILK (SANTAN)

For Curries
Cut shelled coconut into 4 pieces and grate on fine hard grater.
Add $\frac{1}{2}$ cup of water to grated coconut, mix well with hand to get out the thick white juice, squeeze milk through fine strainer into a bowl. This is called the first squeeze, and should be very thick. Add more water, as much as you require, to coconut and repeat process for the second squeeze, and for third squeeze, if necessary. In curries the first squeeze is added last. If you require a thin gravy, remove pan from heat as soon as gravy boils after addition of first squeeze to prevent milk from curdling.

For Cakes and Puddings and Yellow Rice
Remove brown skin of coconut before grating so that you will get white liquid free from brown residue.

If coconut milk is not going to be cooked then use cold boiled water for second squeeze. Make the milk just before it is needed, as coconut milk very quickly becomes rancid.

HOW TO USE CURRY POWDER
Always mix curry powder with a little water to make a thick paste before use.

EGGS
Eggs in recipes in this book are small eggs. If you use the large eggs, use fewer eggs. (6 small eggs = 4 large eggs.)

HOW TO PREPARE BAMBOO SHOOTS FOR COOKING

For Fresh Bamboo Shoots
Remove hard covering and then cut away the skin and sections on the shoot. If large, cut in half. Wash and boil in deep pan of water for at least 2 hours. Drain, wash in cold water before slicing or shredding for dishes to be made.

For tinned bamboo shoots:
Buy the boiled bamboo shoots, not the braised ones. Wash the shoots in cold water and then boil briskly for about 20 minutes to get rid of the tinny flavour. Wash again in cold water before use.

Handy Things for the Kitchen

Brown paper for lining cakes tins
Cake mixing bowls of porcelain – 2 or more of different sizes
Cake Tins various shapes and sizes, of good aluminium:
    2 round sandwich cake tins (20 cm in diameter)
    2 square sandwich cake tins (16cm x 16cm)
    1 Swiss Roll tin
    4 bun tins – 2 trays of 9 hollows each
    1 square cake tin for cakes calling for 375g flour (20 x 20 x 7.5 cm)
    1 square cake tin for cakes 500g flour (31.5 x 31.5 x 7.5 cm)
    Loaf tins, large and small, for Raisin Loaf or cake
    Round Cake tins, large and small
Cake spatula of soft plastic or rubber
Colanders – one large, one medium sized
Cooking thermometer for cake frosting
Egg beater
Egg separator
Jelly moulds of various shapes and sizes
Kitchen scissors
Measuring cups, small and large, of Pyrex or aluminium
Measuring spoons of aluminium
Meat mincer
Orange and lime squeezer
Pastry board and rolling pin
Porcelain bowls and plates, large and small
Pyrex dishes of various shapes, sizes for baking and serving
Skewers – long metal ones, for testing cakes, etc
Tenderiser (metal)

Wire strainers (very fine), 1 large, 1 small
Wire tray for cooling cakes, biscuits, etc
Wooden chopping board

ESSENTIAL EQUIPMENT FOR AN ASIAN KITCHEN

Batu Lesong (Pestle and Mortar)
This is made of granite and is used for pounding sambal blachan, dried prawns, peanuts or curry paste for Malay-style curries that do not call for spices like ketumbar (coriander), jintan puteh (cumin), etc.

Batu Giling (Grinding Stone consisting of a granite slab and roller)
Measurements for medium-sized one:
Slab – 18 x 12 x 4 in (45 x 30 x 10 cm)
Roller – 14 in (35 cm) length, 4 in (10 cm) diameter
The Batu Giling is used when curry paste calls for curry spices like ketumbar (coriander), etc. Grinding is easier and quicker than pounding in a pestle and mortar and you get a finer paste. The Batu Giling should be placed on a brick stand about 28 – 30 in (70 – 75 cm) high, depending on a person's height.

Parut (Grater used for grating coconut, tapioca, fresh ginger, etc.)
There are two types of parut. One type is a sheet of metal finely perforated with holes to gives a rough surface on one side for grating coconut, etc. A medium-sized parut of this kind is about 12 x 5 in (30 x 12.5 cm). The other type is a wooden board measuring 12 x 5 in (30 x 12.5 cm) into which have been driven very fine metal needles on which coconut is grated. As these metal needles sometimes come off, the metal graters are safer to use.

Kwali or wok (Large wide-mouthed, deep cooking pan, sloping down towards the centre.) Very useful for deep fat frying, for frying rice, noodles and vegetables in large quantities, and for steaming foods. The stainless steel kwali is recommended.

Blangah (An earthenware curry pot, deep and a wide mouth, usually provided with a wooden cover.) Some people still use a blangah for curries. As the earthenware tends to retain flavour of curries, keep one for meat and one for fish curries.

Glossary

COMMON VEGETABLES, FRUIT, NOODLES, ETC.

Malay	English
Ayam	Chicken
Babi	Pork
Bangkwang	Yam bean
Bayam	Spinach
Beehoon	Rice vermicelli
Bendi	Ladies fingers
Beras	Rice
Buah betek	Papaya
Daging kambing	Mutton, lamb
Daging lembu	Beef
Daun salad	Lettuce
Dhall	Lentils, split peas
Durian blanda	Soursop
Ikan	Fish
Itek	Duck
Kachang bunchis	French bean
Kachang panjang	Strings bean
Kachang tanah	Peanuts
Kangkong	Water convolvulus
Keladi	Yam

Kelapa	Coconut
Keledek	Sweet potatoes
Ketam	Crab
Ketola	Loofah
Ketola ular	Snake gourd
Kobis	Cabbage
Kobis bunga	Cauliflower
Kway teow	Flat rice noodles
Labu merah	Pumpkin
Limau manis	Oranges
Limau nipis	Local limes larger than calamansi
Limau kesturi	Calamansi
Lobak merah	Carrot
Mee	Noodles from wheat flour
Nanas	Pineapple
Paria	Bitter gourd
Pisang	Banana (some varieties: Hijau, Mas, Rajah, Rastali)
Rebong	Bamboo shoot
Sawi	Chinese cabbage
Susu	Milk
Susu ayer	Evaporated milk
Susu hidop	Fresh milk
Susu manis	Condensed milk
Taugeh	Bean spout
Tauhu	Soft soya bean cake
Taukwa	Hard soya bean cake
Terong	Brinjal
Timun	Cucumber
Timun bulu	Vegetable marrow
Ubi kayu	Tapioca
Ubi kentang	Potato
Udang	Prawns

SPICES, ROOTS AND OTHER INGREDIENTS USED FOR MALAYSIAN CURRIES, CAKES FLAVOURING, ETC

Malay	*English*
Agar-Agar	Gelatine made from seaweed (from Japan)
Asam	Tamarind
Bawang	Onion, leek
Bawang besar	large onion
Bawang merah	Shallots (small red onions)
Bawang puteh	Garlic
Bijian	Sesame
Biji sawi	Mustard seed
Blachan	Shrimp paste
Blimbing	Small green sour fruit used for Malay curries, sambals and Indian pickles
Buah keras	Candlenut
Buah pala	Nutmeg
Buah palaga	Cardamon
Bunga chingkeh	Clove
Bunga lawang	Star anise
Chilli, chabai	Chillies, long red or green peppers
Chilli kering	Dried chillies
Chuka	Vineger
Daun bawang	Spring onion
Daun curry	Curry leaves (karupillay)
Daun kesum	Flavouring leaves, used in laksa or otak-otak
Daun ketumbar	Coriander leaves
Daun pandan	Leaves of small Pandan, used for favouring
Daun seladeri	Celery
Gula batu	Rock sugar, sugar in lumps
Gula melaka	Coconut sugar
Gula pasir	Sifted sugar
Halia	Ginger

Jintan manis	Anise
Jintan puteh	Cumin
Kas-kas	Poppy seeds
Kechup	Soy sauce
Kelapa	Coconut
Kayu manis	Cinnamon
Ketumbar	Coriander
Kunchor	Zeodary, a root not often used; may be used with spices for satay
Kunyit	Turmeric
Lada	Pepper
Langkwas	Greater galangal; ginger root used in Malay curries and sambals
Limau manis	Oranges
Limau nipis	Local limes larger than calamansi
Limau kesturi	Calamansi
Minyak kelapa	Coconut oil
Minyak kachang	Peanut oil
Minyak	Lard
Petis	Prawn paste, used in "rojak"
Rempah	Curry paste, either ground or pounded.
Sambals	Cooked preparation of chillies, blachan, flavouring roots, etc,
Santan	Milky liquid squeezed out of grated coconut after adding water.
Sayor	Vegetable
Serai	Lemongrass
Taucheo	Salted soya beans, brown in colour
Tauyu	Soya sauce
Tempe	Fermented boiled soya beans in flat white cakes, wrapped in green leaves; a rich source of protein, Widely used in Malay food in sayor lemak, sambals and gadoh-gadoh

European Dishes

(many with a Malayan flavour)

Chicken Stew

1 chicken (1½ lb, 680 g),
   cut into pieces
2 tablespoons flour
Salt and pepper, to taste
2 tablespoons butter
2 dessertspoons diced
   onions
¾ cup sliced carrots
Spring onions and celery,
   optional
A small piece of cinnamon
2 cloves
¾ cup button mushrooms

Mix chicken with flour and a little salt and pepper. Put butter in frying pan and fry the pieces of chicken till golden brown. Remove chicken to deep pan.

Fry in remaining butter the diced onions till soft, then add sliced carrots and after a few minutes, pour all into pan with the chicken. Cover chicken with water, add spring onions, celery, salt and spices and allow to simmer till chicken is cooked.

Add mushrooms, cook till gravy reaches consistency required. Thicken gravy with flour, if necessary.

Chicken Pie

Cold chicken stew (see above), enough to fill pie-dish ¾ full.

Short or flaky pastry made from ½ lb (225 g) or ¾ lb (340 g) flour according to size of pie-dish (see page 63 for pastry recipe).

Roast Chicken

1 chicken, about 2 lb (1 kg)
¾ dessertspoons salt and
   ½ teaspoon pepper, or to
   taste
1 dessertspoon flour
2 dessertspoons butter or
   margarine
½ cup water

Bake Stuffing:
1 dessertspoon butter
1 dessertspoon finely diced
   onion
3 chicken livers, boiled and
   coarsely diced
2¼ in (5½ cm) thick slices of
   tinned Spam or chopped
   ham with pork, mashed
   with fork
1 thick slice of bread
   soaked in ½ cup milk
½ teaspoon powdered
   cinnamon
Pepper to taste
A little browning
Salt, if desired
1 beaten egg

Note for this edition:
Used to add a rich, dark colour
to foods, browning sauce is now
available in supermarkets.

Rub salt and pepper inside and outside the chicken and dredge it with the flour, rubbing some inside.

Butter a large pie dish or baking pan. Put chicken in. Put water in pan and place portions of butter on chicken. Bake in oven (180°C, 356°F) for about 1½ hours, or till done and golden brown, turning chicken over when one side browns. Remove chicken in platter. Pour juice in pan into same platter.

Gravy, if required:
Put pie dish in which chicken has been roasted on heat. Add 1 teaspoon flour, stir well into the butter left in pie dish, and when smooth add ¾ cup water, salt and pepper and a little browning for colour. When boiling, pour into gravy dish.

Roasted potatoes:
Boil potatoes in jackets. When cooked, removed skin, and throw potatoes into baking dish when chicken is half done. Alternatively, place peeled raw potatoes in baking dish and roast with chicken.

Heat butter in pan and fry onions till brown. Add liver, mashed Spam, bread, cinnamon, pepper, a little browning for colour, and salt, if desired.

Set aside to cool, before adding beaten egg and mixing well. Put mixture in a well buttered Pyrex dish and put dabs of butter on top.

Bake the stuffing when the chicken is being roasted, but only for an hour or till stuffing sets. Remove from oven and cool, before cutting it into pieces, to serve with the roasted chicken.

For variety:
For Roast Chicken with a cinnamon flavour, mix 1 dessertspoon of powdered cinnamon with the flour to coat the chicken.

Baked Chicken

1 chicken (2 lb, 1kg),
   cut into 12 pieces
Salt and pepper to taste
3 - 4 tablespoons margarine
   or butter
3 tablespoons flour
½ cup water
1½ dessertspoons salt

Rub chicken pieces with salt and pepper. Heat 2 tablespoons butter in large frying pan. Roll the pieces of chicken in the flour and fry in the hot pan till golden brown, turning over when necessary.

Arrange chicken pieces in deep Pyrex dish. Put remaining butter in pan, add leftover flour, then add the water, stirring well to make a thick smooth sauce. Pour this over the chicken.

Cover Pyrex dish and bake in moderate oven for 1½ hours. Remove cover and bake for another 15 minutes.

For variety:
Pork or lamb chop can be used instead of chicken. Flavour with diced mushrooms and green pepper for variety.

Chicken a la King

With Butter Rice and Boiled Long Beans

3 double breasts of chicken
Salt and pepper to taste
2 level dessertspoons butter
1½ level dessertspoons flour
¾ cup diluted evaporated milk
4 red tinned Pimientos cut into ½ in (1¼ cm) pieces
¾ cups tinned sliced mushrooms, broiled in butter, or button mushrooms, sliced coarsely
4 long beans, cut in to 2 in (5 cm) lengths, boiled

Chicken:

Steam chicken with pepper and salt. Remove skin and bones and cut chicken into ½ in (1¼ cm) pieces to make 2 cups.

Heat butter in pan, add flour and mix to a smooth paste. Add milk and stir, adding all ingredients and salt and pepper. When boiling set aside till time to serve.

Mounds of Butter Rice:

Butter small Pyrex cup. Put two or three dessert-spoons freshly cooked hot rice into it, add a little butter, add more rice and press down with a spoon. Repeat process till you have filled the cup. With a knife ease the rice round the edge and turn the mound of rice on to a plate. Make four or five mounds of rice.

Serve Chicken a la King with mounds of butter rice and some boiled long beans.

Duck Pot Roast

1 duck (2½ lb, 1 kg), well
  cleaned
2 tablespoons brandy or
  sherry
6 dessertspoons oil
1 clove garlic, minced
1 dessertspoon diced onions

Ground to a smooth paste:
2 dessertspoons coriander
1 teaspoon peppercorns
1 in (2½ cm) piece cinnamon

1 dessertspoon thick soy
  sauce
1 teaspoon sugar
1½ teaspoons salt

Rub the duck inside and outside with the brandy.

Heat 2 dessertspoons oil in pan, brown garlic, fry
onions and, when soft, add ground spices. Remove
pan from fire, add soy sauce, sugar and 1½ teaspoons salt. Put this mixture inside and outside duck.

Now put the rest of the oil in a deep pan. Fry the
duck to brown the skin a little, turning to brown it
evenly. Add the brandy and spices that may be left in
the dish to 2 cups water, and cook in moderate heat
for about ½ hour. Simmer till duck is dry,
adding more salt, if necessary.

Cut duck into small pieces and serve with Pineapple
and Apple Chutney (see page 187).

Boiled Beef

3 dessertspoons butter
1½ lb (680 g) beef, cut from a
  small round muscle with a
  little fat round it
Salt and pepper
1 tablespoon flour
1½ large onions, diced
4 carrots, cut into 1½ in
  (3cm) lengths
Cinnamon, cloves, celery
  for flavouring

Heat butter in deep pan. Fry beef which has been seasoned with salt and pepper and rolled in flour, till it is well browned.

Add diced onions and after frying for a few minutes, cover meat with water, adding more salt if necessary and carrots, spices and celery. Allow to simmer till meat is tender and gravy reaches the consistency required.

To serve cut beef in thin slices.

Note from this edition:
Use shin beef for this recipe.

Baked Minced Beef

½ lb (225 g) minced beef
1½ dessertspoons flour
2 dessertspoons butter
1 large onion, diced
Salt and pepper to taste
2 oz (55 g) cooked ham, diced
2 oz (55 g) tinned mushroom,
  diced
¾ cups diluted evaporated
  milk
2 eggs beaten

Mix flour with minced beef.

Put butter in frying pan, fry diced onion till soft, add minced beef, stir, adding salt and pepper. When a little brown add ham and mushrooms and remove from fire.

Add milk and when cool add beaten eggs, and more salt and pepper, if necessary.

Put mixture in buttered Pyrex dish, and bake in moderate oven for about an hour till mixture sets and top is a little brown.

For variety:
Substitute minced pork for chicken or beef.

Meat Loaf

1½ lb (680 g) veal or beef,
  minced
¼ lb (115 g) cooked ham,
  minced
2 slices bread, soaked in
  ½ cup milk to soften it
Salt and pepper to taste
3 eggs, slightly beaten
1 large onion, chopped and
  fried slightly
2 dessertspoons butter

Mix all ingredients in the order given except butter. Add more milk, if necessary.

Shape into loaf, put in greased pie dish, put dabs of butter on top. Put into a moderate oven and roast for 1½ hours or till done.

When done remove loaf to platter and slice when required.

Make gravy, if desired, using same recipe as for gravy for Chicken Roast (page 28). If gravy is not wanted serve Meat Loaf with salad.

For variety:
Substitute bacon for ham, or use tinned chopped ham. Before baking put in a few slices bacon or ham across loaf, if you like. If you like pork, use ¾ lb (340 g) rather lean pork.

Stuffed Beef Roll

4 thin slices of rump steak
Salt and pepper to taste
1 or 2 carrots, skinned
1 large onion, coarsely sliced
2 hard boiled eggs
1 red and 1 green chilli,
  seeded
4 or 6 olives, seeded
Flour for dredging
2 - 3 dessertspoons butter
1 large onion, diced
A small piece of cinnamon
2 cloves
2 sprigs of celery

Lay on wooden board the four slices of rump steak, allowing ends to overlap. Sprinkle salt and pepper on meat.

Arrange on meat, for rolling, the carrots, onions, hard boiled eggs, chillies and olives. Sprinkle with more salt and pepper. Make a neat, tight roll (like popia) and secure with thin twine. Dredge meat roll with flour, salt and pepper.

Put butter in deep pan and, when hot, fry the meat roll till brown. Add diced onion and, after a few minutes, cover meat roll with water. Add cinnamon and celery and allow to simmer for 1½ hours, or till roll is properly cooked. Add more salt if necessary and a little flour to thicken gravy.

Roast Beef & Yorkshire Pudding

1½ lb (680 g) beef, rolled
 and tied for roasting
Salt and pepper
½ lb (225 g) good dripping

Yorkshire Pudding:
1 cup flour
Salt
1 cup milk
2 eggs
30g dripping

Beef:
Put beef which has been seasoned with pepper in enamel pie dish or roasting pan and spread on it the dripping. Roast in a hot oven for 30 minutes. Then reduce heat and continue for another hour and a quarter.

Remove from the oven and take beef out of the roasting pan. Set aside the beef in a warm place.

Reserve 2 tablespoons of the dripping to make Yorkshire Pudding. Keep another 2 tablespoons of the dripping in the pan to make gravy.

Yorkshire Pudding:
Add salt to flour, make well in centre and break in eggs. Add a little milk and mix with wooden spoon till smooth. Beat until it bubbles, add the remainder of the milk and allow to stand aside in a cool place for an hour or so. Reserve two tablespoons of the batter to make gravy.

Put the 2 tablespoons of the reserved dripping into a shallow tin. Heat the dripping and pour in the rest of the batter. Bake in very hot oven for about ½ hour. Serve on a hot dish, cut in neat sections.

Gravy:
Place the pan with the two tablespoons of dripping on fire. Add ¾ cup water, salt and pepper to taste and, when boiling, pour in the two tablespoons of pudding batter. Stir into the gravy all the meat juices sticking to sides of pan. Add a few drops of browning (see page 28) if necessary.

To serve:
Remove beef on to a dish, rubbing a little table salt over beef before slicing. Cut into thin slices.

Chilli Con Carne

2 large onions, diced
3 dessertspoons butter
2 fresh chillies, sliced
2 dessertspoons curry
   powder made into a
   paste with a little water
1 lb (450 g) beef, minced
1 small tin cream of tomato
   soup
1 small tin kidney beans
Salt to taste

Fry onions in butter till soft, add chillies and curry paste. After a few minutes add the minced beef. Cook for about 10 minutes and then add the soup and kidney beans, and salt, if necessary. Simmer for about 1 hour.

If you want a hotter dish add more chillies and curry powder.

Minced Beef & Potato Ring

Mashed potatoes:
4 large potatoes
Salt and pepper to taste
½ dessertspoons butter
2 - 3 tablespoons milk

Minced beef:
3 dessertspoons butter
1 large onion, diced
¾ lb (340 g) minced beef
1 dessertspoon flour
Salt and pepper
1 teacup water or milk
A little browning, if needed
Fried croutons

Potatoes:
Remove skin from 4 potatoes and boil potatoes in water till soft. Drain off water. Replace pan on small flame to dry potatoes, adding salt and pepper, butter and milk. Beat till light.

Beef:
Put butter in frying pan. Fried diced onion till soft. Add minced beef which has been mixed with flour, salt and pepper. Stir while frying, and when it is turning brown, add a cup of water or milk. Allow to simmer till meat is cooked, and consistency thick, adding flour to thicken and a little browning.

To serve:
Arrange mashed potato in a platter to form a round or oblong wall about ¾ in (2 cm) high around space to be filled with the meat. Sprinkle over with the fried croutons.

Beef & Chicken Liver Rolls

¼ lb (115 g) minced beef
2 chicken livers, boiled and
   diced
1 thin slice of bread, soaked
   in 2 tablespoons milk
   (diluted evaporated)
1 dessertspoon diced onion,
   fried till soft in a little
   butter or margarine
Salt and pepper to taste
Dash of powdered nutmeg
1 egg
1 dessertspoon butter or
   margarine
6 small rashers bacon

Mix all ingredients, except bacon. Do not use too much salt as bacon is being used.

Divide mixture into 6 portions. Using your hands, make each into a compact roll about 3 in (7½ cm) long. Put a rasher of bacon round each, place rolls in buttered shallow Pyrex dish, put a dab of butter on each, and bake in moderate oven for about 1 hour or till cooked.

Fried Spaghetti

4 dessertspoons butter
1 clove garlic, chopped finely
1 large onion, diced
1 tomato, sliced
1 red fresh chilli, sliced finely
½ lb (225 g) spaghetti, boiled
   in salted water till soft,
   drained
Salt to taste
2 dessertspoons tomato
   sauce
3 eggs, beaten
3 dessertspoons grated
   cheese

Put butter in large frying pan. Fry chopped garlic till golden brown, add diced onion. When soft, add sliced tomato and chilli and spaghetti, stirring well. Add a little salt and tomato sauce.

After about five minutes pour the beaten eggs over the spaghetti and stir. When egg is cooked, add the grated cheese and mix well.

Serve with sauce and meat balls (page 40) or chicken stew (page 27).

Sauce & Meat Balls for Spaghetti

Spaghetti Sauce:
2 dessertspoons butter
2 dessertspoons minced
  onions
1½ cup tinned tomatoes or
  ¾ cup tomato sauce and
  ¾ cup water
¼ cup grated cheese
Salt and pepper to taste
A little sugar to taste

Meat Balls:
1 lb (450 g) minced beef
½ cup soft bread crumbs
⅓ cup grated cheese
1 teaspoon minced parley
A dash of nutmeg
½ teaspoon pepper
2 teaspoons diced onions,
  fried in a little butter
1 clove garlic, minced and
  fried golden brown
Salt to taste
4 tablespoons oil for frying

Sauce:
Heat butter in pan, fry onions till soft, add tomatoes and cheese. Add pepper and salt, if necessary, add sugar.

Meat balls:
Combine all ingredients and shape by half-teaspoons into tiny meat balls. Put aside. Heat 4 tablespoons oil in frying pan. Add meat balls and browns on all sides. Then add in spaghetti sauce.

Rissoles

1 large onion, diced
2 dessertspoons butter
1 dessertspoon flour
3 dessertspoons meat gravy
　or water
Salt and pepper
½ lb (225 g) cold meat, minced
2 eggs
Breadcrumbs
Fat for frying

Fry diced onions in butter till soft, add flour and gravy and stir till thick. Add salt and pepper and pour mixture on the minced meat and stir well. Leave to cool.

Add an egg, mix thoroughly and divide mixture into small portions. Shape each of these rissoles with floured hands. Beat up an egg and dip each rissole first in this and then in breadcrumbs and fry in very hot fat. Cook till rissoles are crisp and golden brown. Drain on brown paper before serving.

For variety:
2 - 3 dessertspoons mashed potato can be added.

Stewed Lamb Chops

8 lamb neck chops
Flour
Salt and pepper
2 - 3 dessertspoons butter
1 large onion, diced
2 - 3 carrots, cut into pieces
A piece of cinnamon
2 or 3 cloves
2 sprigs of celery

Rub salt, pepper and flour on chops. Fry in hot fat till brown and remove from pan. Fry diced onions in pan till a little brown. Add carrots.

Put all ingredients in a deep cooking pot, cover with water, and simmer till meat is cooked.

Add a little flour made into a paste, if a thick gravy is required.

Serve with mashed potato and green peas.

Lamb Roast with Mint Sauce

A leg of lamb (3 lb, about 1.5 kg)
Salt and pepper

Pound finely:
½ clove garlic
2 thin slices ginger
4 small onions

2 dessertspoons butter
A little water

Mint Sauce:
8 sprigs mint leaves
1 dessertspoon boiling water
2 dessertspoons vinegar
½ cup water
Sugar and salt to taste

Remove from lamb excess fat, leaving as much as fat as you like. Rub over with salt and pepper and pounded ingredients.

Put lamb in baking dish, placing on it the butter and add about ¾ teacup water. Roast in moderately hot oven till done (about 2½ hours).

To serve, cut into thin slices and place on platter. Make sauce as for roast chicken (page 28).

Serve with mint sauce, roast potatoes or mashed potatoes and green peas.

Mint Sauce:
Pick, clean and wash mint leaves. Chop very finely, add boiling water, vinegar, ½ cup water, sugar and salt to taste.

Note for this edition:
For a pink Lamb Roast, cook for 2 hours.

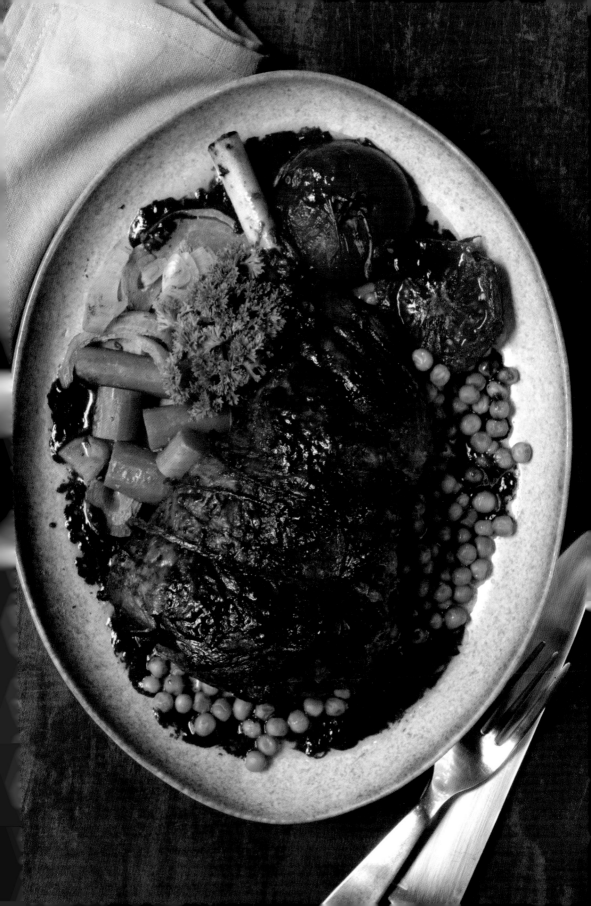

Devilled Crabs

2 tablespoons butter
2 tablespoons flour
⅔ cup milk
Yolks of 2 eggs
Salt and pepper
1½ cups cooked crab meat
½ cups mushrooms, finely
  chopped
1 teaspoon chopped celery
2 crab shells
Breadcrumbs

Make a sauce of butter, flour and milk; when cool, add yolks of eggs, seasoning, crab meat and mushroom.

Wash and trim crab shells, fill with mixture and sprinkle with stale bread crumbs mixed with a little melted butter. Bake in moderate oven till crumbs are golden brown.

For variety:
Add grated cheese to bread crumbs, if you like the flavour.

Fish Cake

1 lb (450 g) fish (ikan karau,
  threadfin) seasoned with
  salt and pepper and
  steamed
1 teacup mashed cooked
  potatoes
½ large onion, diced and
  fried till soft, not brown
2 eggs, beaten
Salt and pepper to taste
1 teaspoon chopped celery
  and spring onions

Mix all the ingredients. Form into round or oblong flat cakes. Dip each in egg white which has been beaten a little, and fry in hot oil till brown.

Deep fat can be used. If you fry in oil that a little more than covers the bottom of a frying pan, turn fish cakes when they brown on one side.

Fish with White Sauce

1 lb (450 g) fish (ikan karau,
   threadfin)
Salt and pepper
1 teaspoon butter

White Sauce:
1 oz (30 g) butter
1 oz (30 g) flour
½ pint (1 cup) milk (diluted
   evaporated or mixture of
   fish stock and milk)
Salt and pepper

1 hard boiled egg, diced

Season fish with a salt and pepper and steam, placing on fish a teaspoon of butter.

To make white sauce, melt butter on low heat, add flour and mix to a smooth paste, adding liquid gradually. When mixture boils, add salt and pepper.

To serve, place steamed fish in platter, pour over it white sauce and sprinkle with diced hard boiled egg.

Baked Prawns with Cheese

16 medium-sized fresh
   prawns
3 large potatoes
1 egg, well beaten
2 dessertspoons grated
   cheese

White Sauce:
1 oz (30 g) butter
1 oz (30 g) flour
½ cup milk
½ cup prawn stock
Salt and pepper

Clean and steam prawns with salt and pepper, reserve stock.

Remove skin from potatoes and boil potatoes in water till soft. Drain off water. Mash. Arrange mashed potato to form a wall along the edge of a shallow Pyrex dish.

To make white sauce, melt butter on low heat, add flour and mix to a smooth paste, adding liquid gradually. When mixture boils, add salt and pepper.

Add beaten egg to white sauce which has been cooled and then mix in the steamed prawns. Pour mixture into space surrounded by mashed potato. Sprinkle on top the grated cheese. Bake for about 40 minutes in moderate oven.

Prawn Fritters

Batter:
1½ cups flour
2 teaspoons baking powder
1 teaspoon salt
⅛ teaspoon paprika
1 egg, beaten
½ cup milk
3 teaspoons water
½ teaspoon grated onion

2 dozen medium-sized
   prawns, shelled and cleaned
Vegetable oil for deep frying

Make a smooth batter of ingredients. Add prawns to this.

Heat oil in pan and, when very hot, drop prawns into it by dessertspoons. When golden brown, drain on paper, and serve.

Batter

For frying prawns and fish

1 cup flour
½ teaspoon baking powder
¼ teaspoon salt
½ cup water or milk
1 egg

Sift flour with baking powder. Mix in salt. Add water or milk gradually, and then eggs which have been beaten till thick.

Baked Fish & Spinach

½ lb (225 g) spinach
Salt and pepper to taste
¾ lb (340 g) steamed fish
1 cup white sauce
   (see page 46)
2 eggs, beaten
1½ dessertspoons grated
   cheese

Boil spinach. Drain and mash a little. Season with salt and pepper

Place spinach in Pyrex dish. Add shredded fish to white sauce (cold) add beaten egg and pour mixture over the spinach. Sprinkle with the grated cheese. Bake in moderate oven for ½ hour or till mixture sets.

Note:
Ikan kurau (threadfin) is recommended. Leave out spinach if you prefer to have the fish without it.

Tomato Fish or Prawns

1 lb (450 g) fish (ikan karau,
  threadfin) or prawns
2 dessertspoons butter
1 large onion, diced
1 red fresh chilli, seeded
  and sliced
1 tomato, diced
2 tablespoons tomato sauce
½ teacup water
Salt and a pinch of sugar

If using fish, cut into two rather thick pieces, season with salt and pepper and fry, not too crisp.

For prawns, shell, clean and season with salt and pepper, and fry in oil or butter.

Put butter in frying pan, fry onions till soft, add chilli and tomato. When cooked, add tomato sauce and water, and salt and sugar to taste. Add fish or prawns and simmer for about ten minutes.

Baked Brinjals and Tomatoes

3 green or purple brinjals
2 dessertspoons butter
1 dessertspoon flour
½ cup diluted evaporated
  milk
Salt and pepper to taste
1 large onion, diced
2 medium sized tomatoes,
  sliced
1 egg
1 oz (30 g) grated cheese

Cut each brinjal into four lengthwise, up to but not through top. Soak in water for 20 minutes. Then plunge into boiling salted water, cover pan and cook till just soft. Drain off all water, using wire sieve. When cool, remove skin, and cut into 3cm lengths.

Make white sauce by putting 1 dessertspoon butter in pan over low heat and, when melted, add flour and mix to smooth paste, then add milk gradually. Add salt and pepper to taste.

Put the other dessertspoon butter in frying pan and fry diced onions till soft and then add sliced tomatoes and a little salt.

Add onions and tomatoes to white sauce, mix in brinjal. When cool add 1 beaten egg and half the grated cheese.

Put mixture in buttered Pyrex dish, sprinkle on the rest of the grated cheese and bake in moderate oven.

Serve with meat loaf or stew.

Salad with Boiled Salad Dressing

1 cucumber, trim off top and
  bottom, scratch through
  skin lengthwise with a fork
  and cut into rather thick
  slices
4 tomatoes, cut into wedges
Pineapple slices, if required
1 small tin asparagus
1 small tin whole beetroot,
  sliced or halved
2 hard-boiled eggs, wedged
A few leaves of lettuce

Boiled Salad Dressing:
1 teaspoon flour
1½ dessertspoons sugar, or
  to taste
Salt and pepper to taste
1 dessertspoon mustard
3 dessertspoons vinegar
¾ cup milk
1 dessertspoon butter

Mix all dry ingredients in pan and make a smooth paste with mustard and a little vinegar. Add milk and bring to boil. Add butter, beat well and put into a small dish.

Arrange vegetables in any way you like on a large platter. Serve with Boiled Salad Dressing.

Date Chutney

Recipe from Sophia Blackmore

1 lb (450 g) preserved dates,
  stoned
½ lb (225 g) preserved ginger
1½ cup vinegar
6 tablespoons brown sugar
4 teaspoons salt
1 saltspoon (¼ teaspoon)
  cayenne
1 teaspoon powdered
  cinnamon
1 teaspoon mustard

Put dates and ginger through mincer.

Boil vinegar and sugar. Pour boiling vinegar over dates and ginger and mash well. Add all other ingredients and pour into bottles.

Note:
For those who prefer a hotter chutney, I would recommend 2 teaspoons chilli powder instead of 1 saltspoon cayenne.

Potato Salad

1 lb (450 g) boiled potatoes,
   diced
1 boiled carrot, diced
½ dessertspoon chopped
   onion, optional
Salt
Boiled Salad Dressing
   (see page 50)

Mix all above ingredients. Serve with cold meats or meat loaf after chilling in refrigerator.

Corn Fritters

1 cup cream-style corn
¾ cup self-raising flour
1 egg, beaten
Salt and pepper
Butter or margarine for frying

Mix all ingredients except butter. Heat a little butter in pan and fry mixture by dessertspoonful, turning over when one side browns.

Serve with meat loaf or baked chicken.

For variety:
Include diced onion and fresh chilli to add flavour to this.

Potatoes fried with Onions

4 dessertspoons butter or
   margarine
2 large onions, finely sliced
6 medium potatoes, boiled
   in jackets, skinned and
   sliced
Salt and pepper to taste

Put 2 dessertspoons butter in a large frying pan and fry onions till soft. Add potatoes, salt and pepper, turning now and then to prevent burning. Add the rest of butter and cook on slow fire till potato is a nice golden brown.

Serve with meat loaf or stew.

For variety:
Add ¼ lb (115 g) chopped ham and 2 eggs beaten well, to make a richer dish.

Tomato Chutney

2 lb (1 kg) red tomatoes

Ground together finely:
20 fresh red chillies, all
    seeded for a mild flavour
2 in (5 cm) length fresh ginger
8 cloves garlic

1½ cups white vinegar
2 dessertspoons salt
2½ cups sugar

Wash tomatoes and put in deep bowl. Pour boiling water over tomatoes and leave to soak for 10 minutes. Drain off water and remove skin and dark spots before cutting tomatoes into ½ in (1¼ cm) pieces.

Mix in deep enamel pan, ground ingredients, vinegar, salt, sugar and cut-up tomatoes.

Boil on slow heat for 1½ hours, stirring occasionally, adding more salt and sugar to suit your taste.

When cool, keep Tomato Chutney in wide-mouthed glass jar so that you can spoon out the chutney.

Note:
Mixed with Chilli Sauce, Tomato Chutney makes a good sweet sour sauce for prawns, fish or pork.

Fresh Tomato Chutney

4 large ripe tomatoes,
    coarsely diced to make 1 cup
1 large onion, finely diced
    (optional)
1 dessertspoon chopped
    local celery
2 fresh green chillies, finely
    chopped (optional)
2 dessertspoons sugar
1 dessertspoon vinegar or
    lime juice
Salt to taste

Mix all ingredients, adding or reducing vinegar and sugar to suit your taste.

Pea Soup with Curry Flavour

3 dessertspoons mixture of
  oil and melted butter
1 dessertspoon diced onion
1½ dessertspoons curry
  power, made into paste
  with two dessertspoons
  water
1 tin green pea soup
1 tin warm water
Fried onions for garnishing

Put oil and butter in deep pan and fry onions. When soft, add curry paste and fry a little. Add the soup which has been mixed with warm water, and allow to simmer slowly.

When serving, garnish with fried onions and add a little lime juice.

Note:
Add more curry power if you want it hotter. This makes a welcome change on a rainy day.

Lentil Soup with Curry Flavour

A Ingredients:
½ lb (225 g) topside beef with
  little fat, cut into pieces
½ cup lentils (red dhall)
2½ - 3 cups water
2 stalks green celery
1 stalk spring onion
1½ teaspoons salt

1 dessertspoon mixture of
  oil and butter
1 dessertspoon diced onions
1½ dessertspoons curry
  powder made into a paste,
  with a little water
Fried sliced onions for
  garnishing
Lime juice

Boil (A) ingredients on slow fire till lentils are thoroughly cooked and broken. Remove beef and pass liquid, which should be quite thick, through a wire sieve, into a bowl, using spoon to press as much of the starch through as possible.

Put the vegetable oil and butter in a deep pan, fry diced onions till soft. Add curry paste, fry a little and then add the thick lentil mixture from (A), and enough water to make a thick soup.

Allow to simmer, adding more salt if necessary. Dice the meat and add to soup, if you want to use the meat.

Add fried onions to garnish each cup of soup with a little lime juice.

Tomato Rice Ring

4 dessertspoons butter, margarine or ghee
1 clove garlic, finely sliced
2 tablespoons diced large onions
1 dessertspoon finely shredded fresh ginger
3 cups rice, washed and drained in colander
2½ cups tomato juice diluted with 2 cups water
3 heaping teaspoons tomato paste
1 dessertspoon salt

Garnishing:
1½ cups boiled frozen peas
Slices of red tomatoes
Hard-boiled eggs, cut into wedges

Heat butter in deep pan and brown garlic. Add onions and when soft, add ginger and rice. Fry a little and then add diluted tomato juice, tomato paste and salt. Stir well, cover pan and cook on medium heat till rice swells and liquid has been absorbed. Lower heat and cook till rice is properly done.

When cooked, just before serving, put rice into a buttered mould, preferably with a funnel, and press down rice to make it stick together.

To serve, unmould rice ring on to a round platter, and garnish space round the ring of rice with alternating sections of green peas, sliced tomatoes, and wedges of hard- boiled eggs.

Serve with curry, Pineapple and Apple Chutney (see page 187), salad or a vegetable dish.

Note:
Use more or less liquid depending on kind of rice used.

Butter Rice

4 dessertspoons butter
1 dessertspoon chopped
onions
2 cups rice, washed and
drained
3 cups water or chicken stock
Salt to taste
¼ - 1 cup raisins
A small piece of cinnamon
and 2 cloves or ¼ teaspoon
powdered cinnamon

Put butter in pan and fry chopped onions till brown; add rice and fry for about two minutes.

Add water or stock, cover and cook on steady fire till water is absorbed. Lower flame and allow to cook slowly in its own steam.

When rice is cooked, add salt, raisins, cinnamon and cloves. Add more butter if desired. Leave pan of rice on slow flame for about ten minutes before serving.

To serve, place rice on platter and decorate top with: Fried onions, blanched almonds fried brown in butter, slices of hard-boiled eggs or thin slices of omelette made without milk.

Serve Butter Rice with curry, chicken roast or meat stew.

Salmon Rice

1 large onion, diced
4 dessertspoons butter
1 fresh red chilli, sliced
2 teacups cold cooked rice
1 cup tinned salmon
Salt and pepper
1½ teacups milk
2 eggs, beaten
1 teacup green peas

Fried diced onions in butter till soft and add the sliced chillies. Remove pan from fire and add the rice and salmon from which bones and skin have been removed. Mix thoroughly, breaking up the salmon.

Add salt and pepper, milk and beaten eggs. Add peas and pour mixture into buttered Pyrex dish and bake in moderate oven for an hour or till mixture is cooked.

Serve with sweet mango chutney or Indian pickles.

Omelette

2 eggs
2 dessertspoons evaporated
  milk
A dash of pepper
A dash of salt
A level dessertspoon of butter

Beat the eggs lightly with fork, just enough to mix the whites and yolks, but no more.

Add the milk, salt and pepper, beating them into the egg.

Heat a frying pan of about 7 - 8 in (17 - 20 cm) over low heat and put the butter in. When very hot, pour egg mixture into pan, then lower heat and cook slowly.

As undersurface sets, lift it slightly with fish slice and tilt the pan to allow uncooked egg to flow underneath to cook. As egg sets, tilt the pan away from you and fold the omelette in three, forming a roll in the pan. Serve immediately.

For variety:
Sprinkle 2 dessertspoons of finely diced cooked ham on the omelette just as it begins to set.

Left over mince meat, meat loaf, mashed sausage meat, minced curry meat, or even green peas can be used to add extra flavour to an omelette. Heat in a separate pan whatever you are using if it comes out of the refrigerator and add to omelette as it begins to set.

If your family likes cheese, sprinkle a dessertspoon of grated cheese on omelette as it sets.

Make a tomato or tomato and cheese omelette sometimes. For this, fry 2 dessertspoons of coarsely diced ripe tomatoes in the fat you are using, adding a pinch of salt. Pour over this the egg and milk mixture and, as it begins to set, sprinkle over a dessertspoon of grated cheese.

Malaysian Omelette

2 eggs
2 dessertspoons cooking oil
   or butter
1 large onion, skinned, cut
   into 2 from top to bottom,
   and finely sliced
1 red fresh chillie, finely
   sliced
Pinch of salt

Beat the eggs. Heat frying pan, put oil in it and, when hot, put in the onions and fry till soft. Add chillies and salt.

Spread out the oinions and chillies and pour the egg mixture and cook slowly.

When egg sets, fold omelette into three, or turn over in sections, thus breaking it into sections.

Notes:
Remove seeds from chilli before slicing if you don't like the omelette hot. A few drops of thick soy sauce improves this omelette.

Scrambled Eggs

2 eggs
2 dessertspoons of
   evaporated milk
A pinch of salt
A dash of pepper
1 dessertspoon margarine
   or butter

Beat eggs well, adding milk, salt and pepper.

Heat butter in frying pan and, when moderately hot, pour in egg mixture and cook on low heat as eggs should be scrambled slowly.

When mixture begins to set, stir with fish slice, turning over cooked portions quickly and scraping it from the sides. Do not overcook and do not use too high heat or else your scrambled eggs will be pieces of tough portions of egg in a watery liquid.

When egg is cooked and has a creamy consistency, remove to platter immediately and serve small portions on buttered toast.

For variety:
Add to the egg mixture any of the following:
2 level dessertspoons of finely minced ham
2 dessertspoons grated cheese
2 dessertspoons finely minced tinned mushrooms

French Toast

2 eggs
6 tablespoons milk, using
    4 tablespoons evaporated
    milk and 2 tablespoons
    water
¼ teaspoon salt
Margarine or butter for
    frying
4 slices stale bread, cut into
    two for easier handling
Jam or Golden Syrup

Beat eggs well, add milk and salt.

Heat a dessertspoon of fat in frying pan. Dip each slice of bread in the egg and the milk mixture and put into the frying pan to brown.

Turn pieces of bread over as one side browns.

Serve hot with jam or Golden Syrup.

Fried Tinned Corn Beef

1 tin corned beef
A little cooking oil, just
    enough to to fry the
    onions, or margarine or
    butter
2 red fresh chillies, finely
    sliced

Break up the corned beef.

Heat pan, put in the oil and, when hot, fry the onions till soft. Add chillies. Then add corn beef, stirring well.

Cook till oil in corned beef is dissolved and the meat is a little dry and brown in parts. Serve with bread and butter.

Savory Sardines or Salmon

2 dessertspoons oil
2 large onions, sliced
3 - 4 chillies, sliced
1 large tin sardines or salmon
1 dessertspoon thick soy sauce
    mixed with ½ cup water
2 - 4 dessertspoons tomato
    sauce, or to taste
1 teaspoon juice from local
    limes, optional

Heat oil in pan and fry onions till soft. Add chillies. Now add the sardines or salmon, fry a little and then add the soy sauce and tomato sauce. Simmer for about 10 minutes, add the lime juice, if desired.

Flaky Pastry

6 oz (170 g) flour
4 oz (115 g) fat, comprising
  1 oz (30 g) butter and
  3 oz (85 g) suet
Cold water for mixing
½ teaspoon salt

Chop or rub in the butter to flour. Mix to a stiff dough with cold water. Roll out to oblong shape.

Chop and mash suet until "spreadable". Divide into 3 parts.

Spread ⅓ of suet on to ⅔ of pastry. Fold into three, the part with no fat on top centre with fat first.

Roll out again. Repeat the previous step twice, using rest of suet.

Fold and roll once without fat. Roll out to required thickness and use.

Notes:
Bake in very hot oven for about 40 minutes, after brushing top with egg and milk. Use for covering meat pies. Fill pie with rich chicken or beef stew that has been cooked. Cover with pasty, leaving hole for steam to escape.

Short Pastry

2 teaspoons sugar, optional
A pinch of salt
½ lb (225 g) flour
4 oz (115 g) butter
1 egg yolk
Cold water for mixing

Add sugar, if using, and salt to flour and rub in the butter lightly with finger tips till flour has consistency of breadcrumbs.

Add beaten egg yolk and a little cold water. Mix to a dough. Roll out to required thickness (fairly thin – less than ¼ in, 6 mm thick.) Bake in hot oven to start. Then lower temperature.

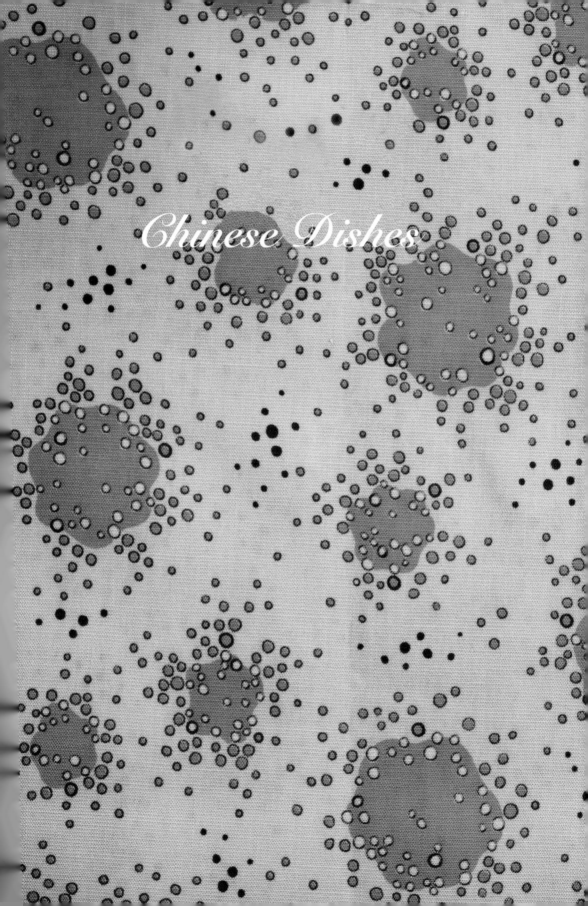

Chinese Dishes

Chicken & Mushrooms

3 dessertspoons cooking oil
1 clove garlic, pounded
1 large onions, sliced
Meat from ½ chicken, cut
  into small slices
Salt and pepper
6 - 8 dried Chinese
  mushrooms, soaked,
  cleaned and sliced
2 - 3 thin slices of ginger
Flour for thickening

Put oil in pan and when hot fry garlic till golden brown. Add sliced onions and fry till soft.

Add chicken and salt and pepper. Fry a little. Add ½ cup water. When chicken is cooked, add mushroom and ginger. Continue cooking for a few minutes. Thicken with a little flour.

Chicken Steamed in Salt

1 chicken (1¼ kati, 1½ lb, 750 g),
  cleaned and drained
2 large sheets grease-proof
  paper
3 - 4 kati (4 - 5½ lb, 2 - 2½ kg)
  salt (not too coarse)

Wrap chicken in two sheets of grease-proof paper. Fill a large enamel pie dish or wok ¾ full of kitchen salt. Place chicken on salt, then cover with more salt till chicken is properly covered. Cover with another dish.

Place on a small fire and cook for 30 minutes. Turn off flame and leave chicken in hot salt, covered, for another 15 or 20 minutes.

To serve, cut chicken into small pieces and serve with Chilli, Ginger and Vinegar Sauce (see page 112), and light soya sauce.

Spiced Roast Chicken

Ground finely together:
2 level dessertspoons coriander
2 cloves
Thumb-nail size piece cinnamon
1 level teaspoon peppercorns

1 teaspoon thick soya sauce
½ teaspoon sugar
4 dessertspoons vegetable oil
  (or 2 oil, 2 butter)
12 small onions, finely ground
2 cloves garlic, finely ground
1 chicken (1½ lb, 680 g)
½ teacup water
Salt to taste

Mix together ¾ teaspoon salt, the ground spices, soy sauce and sugar and rub over the chicken, putting some inside too. Tie some twine around the neck and tie the legs together.

Put oil in kwali or large frying pan and, when hot, fry garlic till golden brown, then add ground onions and fry a little. Put in chicken and fry for 10 minutes or so, turning it over so that it gets brown all round.

Put chicken and fried ingredients into roasting pan, add water and place in moderate oven. Roast for 1½ hours, or till done, turning chicken whenever necessary to make it brown evenly.

For variety:
If you prefer a pot roast, remove chicken after frying, into a deep pan, add 1½ cups water, cover and cook over slow fire for 1 hour or until done. There should be a little gravy to keep the chicken moist. Turn chicken once in a while to make it brown evenly. Cut into small pieces, pouring over chicken the gravy, and serve.

Beef with Mushrooms

4 dessertspoons oil
2 dessertspoons finely sliced
  onions
½ lb (225 g) beef, cut into very
  fine strips or ground
½ cup button mushrooms
1 dessertspoon finely
  shredded fresh ginger
Salt and pepper to taste
1 dessertspoon thick soy sauce
1 dessertspoon cornflour
  mixed with ½ cup
  mushroom juice

Heat 2 dessertspoons oil in pan and brown onions. Remove fried onions to plate. Add the rest of the oil and, when hot, fry the beef till brown. Return the onions to pan, add mushrooms, shredded ginger, salt, pepper and soy sauce. Mix together thoroughly.

Add the cornflour and mushroom juice and continue to cook a few second to thicken.

Spiced Roast Pork

Ground together:
2 tablespoons roasted
  ketumbar (coriander)
½ teaspoon peppercorns
¼ in (½ cm) piece cinnamon
2 cloves

½ teacup small onions,
  ground separately
2 dessertspoons thick soya
  sauce
1½ teaspoons sugar
Salt to taste
1½ katis (2 lb, 900 g) pork
  with skin, rib piece from
  young pig
A little vinegar

Mix ground ingredients with sauce, sugar, and a little salt. Rub over the underside of pork. Place pork in greased baking pan with skin on the top. Brush skin with vinegar and place pork in hot oven.

After about 20 minutes, reduce heat and roast pork for another hour or so till pork is cooked. Remove from oven, cut into pieces and serve with Pickled Radish and Carrot (page 96) or Pickled Kwak Chai (page 96).

Special Roast Pork

1 dessertspoon oil
1 clove garlic, finely ground
4 small onions, finely ground

Ground finely:
1 dessertspoon coriander,
   ground
½ teaspoon peppercorns,
   ground
Small piece cinnamon

½ teaspoon thick soy sauce
   and 1 dessertspoon water
½ teaspoon sugar
1 lb (450 g) roast pork with
   brown cracking, cut into
   pieces
Salt, if desired

Heat oil in pan, brown ground garlic and onions, add ground spices, fry a little and then add the soy sauce and sugar.

Mix the cut pork up with this paste, adding salt if necessary. Put into baking pan and put in slow oven for 10 minutes.

Serve with pickled vegetables (page 96).

Note:
This is easy to make and saves you the trouble of roasting the pork.

Babi Tauyu
Pork in Soy Sauce

1 dessertspoon oil
2 cloves garlic, bruised
1 lb (450 g) pork with some
   fat and skin, cut into
   pieces, not too small
4 dessertspoons thick soy
   sauce
4 cups water
A piece of cinnamon
2 cloves
Salt to taste

Heat oil and brown garlic. Add pork and fry for 5 minutes, add soy sauce and water. Cover pan and simmer till pork is tender, adding more water if necessary. Add spices and salt and allow to cook till gravy reaches consistency required.

For variety:
Add shelled hard boiled eggs after pork is tender.
Add shelled chestnuts with the pork.

Sweet Sour Pork

½ lb (225 g) pork fillet cut into
   slices ½ in (1¼ cm) thick

Mix together:
½ teaspoon seasoning powder
2 teaspoons light soy sauce
2 teaspoons sherry
½ teaspoon crushed fresh
   ginger
½ teaspoon salt

Batter:
2 beaten eggs
1 tablespoon flour
1 teaspoon cornflour
Salt to taste

Combine the mixed ingredients and the pork. Allow pork to absorb all the juice.

Dip pork slices in batter and fry in hot deep fat oil till nicely browned. Drain on paper.

To serve, put fried pork in platter and pour over the sweet sour sauce (see below).

Sweet Sour Sauce

Mix together:
½ cup water
½ cup sugar
¼ cup vinegar, or to taste
1 dessertspoon cornflour
1 teaspoon thick soy sauce

1 small tomato cut into
   wedges
1 dessertspoon shredded
   sweet gherkins
1 teaspoon shredded
   preserved sweet ginger

Put the mixed ingredients in a pan and bring to a boil on slow fire, stirring all the time. When mixture thickens and boils, add tomatoes, gherkins and ginger.

Pork in Tomato and Chilli Sauce

1 lb (450 g) pork steak, cut
  into 1cm slices
2 cream crackers, rolled to
  make fine crumbs
Salt to taste

Vegetable oil or margarine
2 large onions, sliced
1 teaspoon shredded ginger
1 large tomato sliced

*Mixed with water
  to make a cup:*
½ cup tomato sauce
2 tablespoons chilli sauce

Sugar, if desired

Tenderise the pieces of pork with metal tenderiser. Coat these with crumbs and salt. Heat oil in large frying pan, put in the crumbed pork pieces and fry till slightly brown on both sides.

Add water and cook in covered pan till pork is tender, adding water when necessary. When pork is soft and all water has evaporated, add onions, ginger and tomatoes, and cover pan.

When onions are soft, add the tomato and chilli sauce mixture, stir well and simmer till gravy is of required consistency, adding more salt and a little sugar, if necessary.

Pig Liver Balls

½ kati (10½ oz, 300 g) pig liver
About a teacupful of
   vegetable oil
2 cloves garlic, ground
¾ cup small onions, ground

Ground together:
2 tablespoons roasted
   ketumbar (coriander)
½ teaspoon peppercorns

2 tablespoons thick soya
   sauce
1 dessertspoon sugar, or to
   taste
1 teaspoon salt, or to taste
¾ kati (1 lb, 450 g) lean pork,
   minced
4 - 6 tahils (5 - 8 oz, 150 - 225 g)
   pork caul*

* This is the lacy, fatty
membrane encasing the
internal organs of a pig. It
is called Mng Sek Yew in
Teochew and Chee Mong
Yow in Cantonese.

Boil the pig liver just enough so you can cut it easily. Dice finely.

Put two dessertspoons oil in frying pan. Fry garlic till brown. Add the ground onions and fry on slow fire till well browned, then add the ground ketumbar and pepper and fry a little. Add sauce, sugar, and salt and mix thoroughly.

Remove pan from fire and add in liver and pork, mixing it well with the ingredients. Add more salt, if necessary.

Cool and make it into balls smaller than a walnut using fingers. Wrap each ball in the thin membrane allowing ends to overlap securely to prevent skin from opening during frying.

Fry balls in shallow oil in frying pan till brown, turning them as they brown. Fire should not be too strong.

Serve with Pickled Radish and Carrot (page 96) or Pickled Kwak Chai (page 96).

For variety:
Substitute chicken livers for pig liver.

Chap Chye

4 dessertspoons oil
3 clove garlic, minced
2 teaspoons taucheo (salted
 soya beans) pounded
½ lb (225 g) pork or chicken,
 cut into pieces
½ lb (225 g) fresh prawns,
 shelled and cleaned
Salt to taste

1 oz (30 g) tauhu kee (dried
 beancurd skin), cut into
 3 cm lengths and soaked in
 warm water
1 oz (30 g) kim chiam (lily
 buds), stalks removed and
 soaked in warm water
1 oz (30 g) dried mushrooms,
 stalks removed and
 soaked in warm water
½ oz (15 g) bokgi (black wood
 fungus), stalks removed
 and soaked in warm water
½ oz (15 g) soohoon (transparent
 vermicelli), cut into 1½ in
 (3 cm) lengths and soaked
 in cold water
¼ lb (115 g) cabbage, cut into
 pieces
¼ lb (115 g) boiled bamboo
 shoot, sliced
3 cakes taukwa (hard bean
 curd), cut into small pieces
 and fried a little
½ chicken seasoning cube

Heat oil in deep pan, brown garlic, and the fry the pounded taucheo a little. Add the pork or chicken and, after a few minutes, add a little water.

When the meat is half cooked, add prawns and salt. Add the tauhu kee, kim chiam, dried mushrooms, bokgi and 2 cups of water and salt and allow to simmer for about 45 minutes.

Now add the cabbage, bamboo shoot and tauhu, and continue simmering till cabbage is done. Add more water, if necessary, and half of a chicken cube.

Steamed Fish

1 medium-sized ikan bawal
  (pomfret) or ikan krapu
  (grouper) (1¼ lb, 570 g),
  clean and make 2 cuts on
  each side to bone
Salt and pepper to taste
1 teaspoon cornflour
2 dessertspoons light soy
  sauce
1 large onion, coarsely sliced
6 large Chinese mushrooms,
  sliced after washing and
  soaking in water
1 teaspoon finely shredded
  fresh ginger
1 tablespoon shredded carrot
2 sprigs celery, whole

Rub salt and pepper inside and outside fish, and place in the dish. Mix flour and soy sauce to a smooth paste and add in onion, mushroom, ginger, carrot and celery.

Mix thoroughly and then spread over top of fish. Steam for about ½ to ¾ hour.

Before serving remove the celery sprigs.

Steamed Crab with Chilli-Apricot Sauce

4 medium-sized crabs

Mix together:
**3 tablespoons finely shredded
  ginger
3 teaspoons cornstarch
2 dessertspoons thin soy sauce
2 tablespoons gin
1 teaspoon sugar
1 teaspoon salt**

Chilli-Apricot Sauce A
**10 fresh chillies, seeded, and
  pounded not too finely
½ in (1¼ cm) piece fresh
  ginger, pounded finely
⅓ cup white vinegar mixed
  with ⅔ cup water
Sugar and salt to taste
¼ cup apricot jam, apricot
  broken with a fork**

Chilli-Apricot Sauce B
**½ cup Chilli Sauce 2
  (page 193)
½ cup or more cold water
Sugar and salt
Apricot jam**

Kill crabs and remove all unwanted parts and wash thoroughly. Cut each crab into 4 parts and crack shell a little. Put in large deep enamel dish.

Mix the mixture thoroughly with the crabs. Stand a base in some water in a kwali (wok). Place the dish of crabs on this. Cover kwali and steam for half an hour or till crabs are cooked.

Arrange crabs in large platter and garnish with parsley or sprigs of coriander leaves. Serve with your choice of Chilli-Apricot Sauce below.

Chilli-Apricot Sauce:
Mix all the sauce ingredients, adding or reducing ingredients to suit your taste.

Fish with Sweet Sour Sauce

1½ lb (750 g) fish, red fish like snapper or bawal (pomfret), fried nice and crisp, or steamed

Sweet-sour sauce
2 tablespoons vinegar
4 tablespoons water
1½ tablespoons sugar
1½ teaspoons cornflour
½ teaspoon thick soy sauce
Salt to taste

Mix all ingredients and boil.

Add 1 dessertspoon each of chopped spring onions and celery, ½ teaspoon shredded ginger and sliced green or red chillies.

To serve, put fish in platter. Pour sauce over it.

For variety:
A dessertspoon of finely shredded carrot or radish or both can be added to this sauce.

Fish in Soy Sauce & Taucheo

4 dessertspoons oil
15 small onions, finely sliced
2 cloves garlic, finely minced
1 teaspoon taucheo (salted soya bean), pounded
1 teaspoon finely shredded fresh ginger
4 red chillies, coarsely sliced
1 teaspoon thick soy sauce mixed with ½ cup water
1 lb (450 g) of any fresh fish, parang (wolf herring), kurau (threadfin) or selah (scad), fried golden brown
Vinegar or lime juice to taste
Salt to taste

Heat oil in pan, brown garlic, add onions and fry till soft. Add taucheo, fry a little, then add ginger, chillies and sauce.

Put in the fish, and allow to simmer in gravy till a little thick. Add vinegar or lime juice, and salt to suit your taste.

Crab, Bamboo Shoot & Shark's Fin Omelette

1½ lb (750 g) fresh bamboo
  shoot
3 tablespoons vegetable oil
2 cloves garlic, finely minced
½ lb (225 g) pork, boiled and
  shredded
1½ cups stock from pork or
  pork bones
Salt and pepper to taste
½ lb (225 g) fresh prawns,
  shelled, cleaned, diced and
  fried in a little oil
2 rounds of shark's fins,
  soaked in warm water and
  thoroughly cleaned
4 eggs, slightly beaten
1 teacup cooked crab meat
  from 1 large crab
Coriander leaves

Boil bamboo shoot for 3 hours before shredding finely to give 2 teacups worth.

Heat oil in pan, fry garlic till golden brown and add shredded pork. After about 5 minutes add shredded bamboo shoot, stock and salt and pepper to taste.

When mixture is a little dry, add fried diced prawns, stir well and then add shark's fins. Stir well and pour the beaten eggs over the mixture. As eggs harden stir mixture gently and add crab meat. The consistency of dish should be dry.

Place mixture on platter, garnish with coriander leaves and serve.

Note:
If you wish to save time use tinned bamboo shoot. Wash and boil for 10 minutes before shredding.

Simple Fried Vegetables

3 dessertspoons oil
3 cloves garlic, minced
½ lb (225 g) prawns or sliced
    pork, or a little of each
Salt and pepper to taste
Seasoning powder (optional)

*Any of these vegetables
and ingredients:*
1 lb (450 g) French beans
3 pieces taukwa (hard soya
    bean cake), coarsely sliced
    and fried a little first
1 lb (450 g) ketola (snake
    gourd), for this add 2
    beaten eggs at the end
1 lb (450 g) of any kind leafy
    vegetable
1 lb (450 g) long Chinese
    cabbage

Heat oil, brown garlic, add pork and a little water. When cooked add prawns and after 3 minutes add the vegetables, salt, pepper and seasoning powder.

Cover pan for a few minutes, then stir and serve.

Notes:
Do not overcook vegetables. Add stock if you like vegetables a little moist.

Crab & Loofah Omelette

1 loofah (ridge gourd, si gua),
    skin removed, pulp shredded
2 tablespoons lard or
    vegetable oil
1 clove garlic, pounded or
    minced
1 large onion, coarsely sliced
1½ teacups cooked crab meat
    from 2 medium crabs
Pepper and salt to taste
4 - 6 eggs, slightly beaten
Coriander leaves
Red chilli, seeded, shredded

Heat a little oil in pan and fry shredded loofah till a little soft. Remove to plate and drain away liquid.

Heat rest of oil in pan, fry garlic till golden brown, and then add sliced onions. When soft, add loofah, stir in the crab meat, adding salt and pepper, and then pour in the beaten eggs.

As omelette hardens, turn over mixture gently, a portion at a time, till egg is properly cooked.

Place on platter, garnish top with coriander leaves and shredded red chillies.

Mixed Vegetables Dish

2 dessertspoons cooking oil
2 cloves garlic, finely minced
½ kati (10½ oz, 300 g) fresh
  prawns, shelled, cleaned
  and diced
1 large carrot, thin sliced
  lengthwise in pieces 1½ in
  (3 cm) long
4 large dried mushrooms,
  soaked in water, washed
  and thinly sliced
16 French beans, cut into
  1½ in (3 cm) lengths
3 tablespoons frozen green
  peas
½ cup water
Salt and pepper to taste
¾ lb (340 g) cauliflower, cut
  into pieces
1 small green pepper, cut into
  pieces
2 tablespoons tinned
  mushrooms, halved
1 level teaspoon cornstarch
  mixed with 1 dessertspoon
  light soy sauce and
  ½ teaspoon of seasoning
  powder

Put oil in pan. When hot fry garlic till brown. Add prawns, stirring well. After a few minutes, add carrots, mushrooms, French beans and frozen peas, adding ½ cup water and salt.

Cover pan for 5 minutes. Then add the cauliflower, green pepper and tinned mushrooms and cook for another 10 minutes.

Remove cover, stir, and if vegetables are sufficiently cooked to suit your taste, add the cornstarch, seasoning powder and soya sauce paste. Stir well and serve. The vegetables should not be overcooked.

For variety:
Use shredded meat from breast of chicken instead of prawns, or use both.

Leave out prawns and chicken and make a purely vegetable dish.

Shredded Cabbage & Soohoon

3 dessertspoons cooking oil
2 cloves garlic, finely minced
10 medium fresh prawns,
  shelled, cleaned and diced
Salt and pepper to taste
1 lb (450 g) cabbage, finely
  shredded
1 oz (30 g) soohoon (transparent
  vermicelli), cut into 3 cm
  lengths and soaked in cold
  water
2 eggs, well beaten

Heat oil in pan, fry garlic till golden brown, add diced prawns and a little salt and pepper. Add shredded cabbage, stir well, cover pan and cook for 10 minutes or till soft.

Remove cover, add soohoon and when vegetable is a little dry, add beaten eggs, stirring gently till eggs hardens.

For variety:
Use 1 medium-sized vegetable marrow, sliced and shredded. This vegetable cooks quickly. Give it less time than you do to cabbage.

Use ½ lb (225 g) salted vegetable (kiam chye) very finely shredded.

Leave out soohoon if you do not like it.

Vegetables in Taucheo

3 dessertspoons oil
2 cloves garlic, minced
10 small onions, sliced
2 teaspoons taucheo (salted
  soya beans), pounded to a
  paste
2 - 4 red chillies, pounded to
  a fine paste or coarsely
  sliced
12 medium-sized prawns,
  cleaned and halved
1 lb (450 g) of any of these
  vegetables, cut into pieces:
  long beans, French beans,
  ladies fingers or bitter gourd
½ cup water
Salt to taste

Heat oil in pan. Brown garlic, add onions and, when soft, add taucheo and chilli paste. Add prawns and, when cooked, add vegetable and ½ cup water. Stir and cover pan and cook for 5 minutes.

Remove cover and continue cooking till vegetable reaches degree of softness you like.

Bean Curd, Green Peppers & Green Beans

3 dessertspoons oil
1 clove garlic, minced
2 fresh red chillies, ground to
  a paste
4 white taukwa (hard soya
  bean cake), each cut into
  16 cubes
Salt to taste
1 cup frozen peas, boiled
1 green pepper, cut into small
  squares

Mixed into a smooth paste:
2 dessertspoons light soya
  sauce
2 dessertspoons vinegar
½ teaspoon seasoning powder
1 teaspoon sugar
1 dessertspoon cornflour
2 dessertspoons water

Heat oil in pan and brown the garlic. Add chilli paste, frying for few seconds. Add bean curd cubes and a little salt, and fry for about 5 minutes.

Add green peas and green pepper. When thoroughly mixed, add seasoning mixture, stirring gently. Cover pan for a few minutes to cook green pepper just a little.

Taukwa in Taucheo

2 dessertspoons oil
2 cloves garlic, pounded
1½ teaspoons taucheo (salted
  soya beans), pounded not
  too finely
12 medium-sized fresh
  prawns, shelled, cleaned
  and diced
6 pieces taukwa (hard soya
  bean cake), coarsely sliced
¾ cup water
Salt to taste
4 chillies, coarsely sliced
2 dessertspoons chopped
  celery
2 dessertspoons chopped
  spring onions

Heat oil in pan, brown garlic, then add taucheo, fry a little, and then add prawns. When cooked, add the taukwa, stir gently and add ¾ cup water and salt. When gravy reaches consistency required, add chillies and chopped celery and spring onions.

For variety:
Add coarsely shredded French beans and leave out taucheo if you don't care for the flavour.

Leave out prawns and add diced ikan kurau (threadfin).

Baked Tauhu

2½ teacups tauhu puteh (soft
   bean curd)
2 dessertspoons vegetable oil
1 clove garlic, chopped
1 teaspoon pounded taucheo
   (salted soya bean)
3 dessertspoons chopped
   fresh prawns
Salt and pepper
2 eggs, slightly beaten
1 dessertspoon chopped
   spring onions
1 dessertspoon chopped
   celery

Put tauhu puteh in a wire sieve, breaking it up a little and allowing water to drain out.

Put oil in pan and, when hot, fry garlic till brown. Add taucheo, fry a little and then add chopped prawns and a little salt.

When cooked, remove pan from fire, add the tauhu puteh, stir well and then mix in the eggs. Add pepper and chopped spring onions and celery.

Bake in moderate oven for about 40 minutes or till mixture sets like a custard.

Note:
Leave out the taucheo if you do not care for the flavour.

8 katis (10½ lb, 4.8 kg) fresh
  rebong (bamboo shoot)
2 katis (2½ lb, 1.2 kg)
  bangkwang (yambean)
1 teacup oil
10 cloves garlic, pounded
2 dessertspoons taucheo
  (salted soya beans), more
  if you like, pounded
2½ katis (3⅓ lb, 1½ kg)
  prawns, cleaned and diced*
2 katis (2½ lb, 1.2 kg) pork,
  boiled and shredded*
Salt to taste
4 - 5 teacups prawn and pork
  stock
10 pieces taukwa (hard soya
  bean cake), shredded fine
  and fried a little†

* ½ kati (10½ oz, 300 g)
  prawns and ¼ kati (5 ¼ oz,
  150 g) pork to be set aside
  for garnishing.
† 1 teacupful fried taukwa
  to be a side for garnishing

Garnishing:
½ kati (10½ oz, 300 g) diced
  prawns (from filling), fried
  with salt and pepper
¼ kati (5 ¼ oz, 150 g) shredded
  boiled pork (set aside from
  filling), fried with a little
  soya bean sauce and pepper
1 teacupful fried shredded
  taukwa (from filling)
2 eggs made into omelette
  and shredded
1 teacup cooked crab meat,
  fried a little with salt and
  pepper

Popia

For 16 - 18 people

½ cup pounded garlic, fried
   golden brown and broken
   into crumbs§

§ To prevent garlic sticking
   together during frying,
   wash and drain pounded
   garlic before frying.

Vegetables:
½ kati (10½ oz, 300 g) lettuce,
   each leaf halved, centre
   stems removed
2 cucumbers, skinned, cored
   and shredded
½ kati (10½ oz, 300 g) beansprouts, scalded
4 bundles of coriander leaves
Leaves from a few sprigs of
   the larger coriander leaves

Other ingredients:
1½ kati (21 oz, 900 g) large
   popia skin (from shop)
½ kati (10½ oz, 300 g) small
   popia skin (from shop)
1¼ kati (1½ lb, 750 g) tee chio
   (a kind of treacle) (from
   shop), boiled before use
30 - 40 fresh red chillies,
   finely ground
2 dessertspoons mustard
   made into paste with water
Pounded fresh garlic
   (optional)

Egg skin:
1 cup flour
6 eggs
1¼ cups water
A little salt
Vegetable oil

Boil the rebong for 3 - 4 hours the day before popia
is made.

Shred rebong and bangkwang.

Put oil in pan and, when hot, fry pounded garlic till
golden brown. Add pounded taucheo and fry a little.
Add diced prawns and, when cooked, add shredded
pork.

Cook for about 10 minutes, and then add rebong. Stir
well, adding salt and some prawn and pork stock.

Cover pan, and allow to simmer for an hour. Add
shredded bangkwang and more stock, and leave to
simmer for another hour.

Add the fried taukwa. Allow to simmer until mixture
is just moist and oil begins to show as you stir.

Egg Skin

Put flour in basin, beat in eggs, one by one, then add
water, a little at a time. Add salt. Beat till smooth.

Heat frying pan, brush with oil, and pour enough
batter to cover pan. When cooked, edges will curl and
begin to leave pan.

Turn on to the back of a bread plate which has
been place on a meat plate, face to face.

Pai Tee

Shells (makes 50):
1 cup flour
1 egg
¾ cup water
Salt and pepper
A small deep pan of hot oil
Pie tee mould

Filling:
4 dessertspoons oil
6 cloves garlic, minced
**1 teaspoon pounded taucheo
   (salted soya beans)**
**½ kati (10½ oz, 300 g) pork,
   boiled and shredded finely**
**½ kati (10½ oz, 300 g) prawns,
   diced**
Stock from pork
Salt
**3 teacups finely shredded
   bamboo shoot**
**1 teacup finely shredded
   bangkwang (yambean)**
**4 pieces taukwa (hard soya
   bean cake), shredded
   finely and fried a little**

Garnishing:
**½ cup cooked crab meat,
   shredded**
**Omelette from 2 eggs, finely
   diced**
**Coriander leaves, coarsely
   chopped**
Chilli and vinegar sauce

Sauce (mix together):
2 tablespoons vinegar
2 tablespoons water
**4 fresh red chillies, finely
   ground**
Salt and sugar to taste

Shells:
Pour flour in bowl. Add beaten egg, mix gradually, adding water to make a smooth batter.

Heat oil in pan. Heat Pie Tee mould in oil, then remove it and dip it in batter and place mould in oil till shell gets a little brown and loose. Remove and drain on paper.

When slightly cool, place in bottle or tin and keep covered to keep shells crisp till required.

Filling:
Put oil in pan and, when hot, fry garlic till brown. Add taucheo, fry a little, add shredded pork, and after a few minutes, add the prawns. When cooked add a little stock and salt.

Add bamboo shoot, stir, and add more stock. Leave to boil for a few minutes, then add bangkwang and leave to cook.

Add taukwa. Stir. Simmer till mixture is nearly dry.

To serve:
Fill Pie Tee shells with mixture. Decorate top of each with crab meat, omelette and coriander leaves. Serve with freshly prepared chilli and vinegar sauce.

Note:
Instead of using a combination of bamboo shoot and bangkwang, you may use 4 teacups of bamboo shoots.

Fried Popia

**4 - 6 cups of cold popia filling
(page 91)**
16 - 20 popia skins (from shop)
1 egg white, beaten a little
Oil for frying

Separate popia skins. Lay popia skin on a wooden board, put on it 2 dessertspoons popia filling (or more depending on size of popia skin).

Roll up quite tightly like a sausage and seal edges with egg white. Repeat process till all filling is used up.

Heat oil ($\frac{1}{2}$ in, $1\frac{1}{4}$ cm deep) in large frying pan. Fry rolls, turning over when one side browns.

Serve with Chilli, Ginger and Vinegar Sauce (page 112)

Note:
This is a good way of using up your leftover popia filling.

Pickled Radish & Carrot

2 radish
1 carrot
1 teaspoon salt
Red chillies, sliced
Sugar and vingar to taste

Skin the radishes and carrot, then cut into very thin slices.

Add a teaspoonful of fine salt. When vegetables are soft, add a little water and squeeze out all juice.

Add a few slices of fresh chillies, sugar and vinegar to taste.

Pickled Kwak Chai

½ kati (10½ oz, 300 g) picked kwak chye (salted preserved mustard greens)
Salt
¼ teaspoon finely shredded ginger
1 teaspoon mustard powder
Vinegar, sugar and salt to taste

Wash picked kwak chye thoroughly. Cut leaves into 1 x 3 in (2½ x 7½ cm) pieces and slice stalks lengthwise in 2 in (5 cm) lengths, very thinly.

Sprinkle a little fine salt on cut up vegetable and leave for ½ hour. Then squeeze out water.

Add ¼ teaspoon finely shredded ginger, 1 teaspoon mustard powder, vinegar, sugar and salt to taste.

Beehoon Ah Foon's Style

½ cup vegetable oil

2 cloves garlic, ground

½ kati (10½ oz, 300 g) prawns, cleaned and halved

½ kati (10½ oz, 300 g) fish (ikan kurau, threadfin), cut into pieces

6 dried mushrooms, soaked in water and then sliced

Ground together:

6 fresh red chillies, seeded

½ cup onions

¾ kati (1 lb, 450 g) beehoon (rice vermicelli), scalded well, washed in cold water and drained

Salt to taste

½ kati (10½ oz, 300 g) taugeh (beansprouts), cleaned

3 eggs, beaten

2 dessertspoons chopped spring onions

2 dessertspoons chopped celery

2 bundles coriander leaves

Put 2 dessertspoons oil in small pan and, when hot, fry the ground garlic till brown. Add prawns and, when cooked, add fish. Cook for ten minutes, add mushroom and salt to taste. Put aside for later use.

In a large, shallow pan (kwali) put the remaining oil and fry the pounded chillies and onions until well cooked. Add beehoon, stir well, adding salt.

Make a well in centre and put in taugeh. Cover with beehoon and after five minutes stir taugeh into beehoon. Push beehoon to one side and fry the beaten eggs, a little at a time till all has been used up, lifting the omelette in pieces as it cooks on to the beehoon. Add the chopped spring onions and celery and stir well.

Just before serving, add to beehoon half of the mixture of fried prawns etc, keeping the other half to spread over the top. Garnish with coriander leaves.

For variety:

Instead of fish, pork or chicken can be used.

Egg Noodles Fried with Vegetables

6 oz (170 g) egg noodles
4 dessertspoons oil
2 cloves garlic, minced
1 teaspoon taucheo (salted
   soya beans), finely pounded
1 lb (450 g) fresh medium-
   sized prawns, shelled,
   cleaned and halved
1 dessertspoon salt
Pepper to taste
2 teacups chicken or pork
   stock
1 cup shredded cabbage
½ shredded carrot
½ cup shredded French beans
2 cups bean sprouts

Garnishing:
Shredded omelette from 1 egg
Coriander leaves
1 dessertspoon finely sliced
   fresh red chillies

Put the noodles in deep pan, pour boiling water to more then cover them, stir well with wooden spoon or chopsticks and allow to soak for about 10 minutes to soften them. Drain water away, add cold water to noodles and pour into colander to allow water to drain away. Put noodles aside for use later.

Heat oil in large frying pan or kwali, if you have one, and brown garlic. Add the taucheo, fry a little and then add prawns and a dessertspoon salt and some pepper. After five minutes, add stock and, when boiling, add all the vegetables except beansprouts. Cover pan for about 5 minutes.

Then add noodles and mix well with the vegetables. Add beansprouts, stirring them into the noodles. Add more salt and pepper if necessary. This is a dry dish.

Put noodles in a large platter. Garnish top with omelette, coriander leaves and sliced chillies.

For variety:
Pound 1 fresh red chillies with the taucheo if want this dish hot.

Serve with Pineapple and Cucumber Sambal (See page 131).

Fried Kway Teow

Fried Rice Noodles

4 tablespoons vegetable oil or
  freshly made lard
4 cloves garlic, pounded

Ground together:
6 fresh red chillies, seeded
10 small onions

½ kati (10½ oz, 300 g) prawns,
  cleaned and halved
¾ kati (1 lb, 450 g) kway teow,
  scalded and drained just
  before using
Salt to taste
½ kati (10½ oz, 300 g) taugeh
  (beansprouts), cleaned
2 tablespoons kuchai (chives),
  cut into ½ in (1 cm) lengths
1 dessertspoon light soya
  sauce
4 eggs, beaten

Put oil in pan (kwali) and fry pounded garlic till
golden brown. Add ground chillies and onions and,
when well cooked, add prawns and stir well.

After prawns are cooked, add kway teow and salt
and stir well. Make a well in the centre, put in taugeh
and kuchai and add a little more salt, and cover with
kway teow. After about five minutes, stir taugeh into
the kway teow and, when properly mixed, add soya
sauce.

Put kway teow to one side, pour in egg, a little at
a time to cook till all has been used up, lifting the
omelette in pieces as it cooks onto the kway teow. Stir
well before serving.

Note:
Leave out the kuchai if you do like the flavour.

Mah Mee

6 dessertspoons oil
4 cloves garlic, pounded
½ dessertspoon pounded
    taucheo (salted soya beans)
½ kati (10½ oz, 300 g) prawns,
    cleaned and halved
½ kati (10½ oz, 300 g) boiled
    pork, shredded
2½ teacups stock from pork
    bones and prawn shells
⅓ kati (7 oz, 200 g) taugeh
    (beansprouts), cleaned
1 kati (21 oz, 600 g) mah mee
    (fresh yellow noodles)

Garnishing:
1 dessertspoon fried onions
Slices of red and green
    chillies
1 dessertspoon chopped celery
1 dessertspoon chopped
    spring onions
2 bundles coriander leaves
    (if desired)
2 cucumbers, peeled and
    shredded
Omelette from 2 eggs,
    shredded finely
1 cup shredded crab, fried
    with pepper and salt

Heat oil in pan. Fry pounded garlic till golden brown. Add taucheo, then prawns and fry a little.

Add shredded pork and a little salt. Add stock. When boiling add beansprouts. Put mah mee on top of beansprouts.

After 5 minutes or so, stir well, using big fire to prevent mee from becoming soggy. Add more salt if necessary.

Put mah mee on platter. Garnish top.

Note:
The mee used here is the type sold by vegetable stalls.

For variety:
Chicken can be used instead of pork.

Mee Suah Soup

3 dessertspoons oil
2 cloves garlic, minced
10 fresh prawns, diced
Salt to taste
4 cups stock or water
2 ketola (snake groud),
 skinned and cut into small
 pieces
4 bundles mee sua (Chinese
 vermicelli), soaked in cold
 water just before use
2 tablespoons diced ikan
 kurau (threadfin)
Pepper to taste
2 eggs, beaten
Coriander leaves, spring
 onions and celery for
 garnishing
1 tablespoon browned sliced
 onions

Heat oil in pan. Brown garlic, add prawns and little salt. Add water or stock. When boiling add ketola, cover pan for a few minutes. Add mee sua and diced fish, pepper and more salt if necessary.

Just before serving, add beaten eggs and stir a little. Garnish with coriander leaves, spring onions, celery and browned onions.

For variety:
Substitute small pork and crab or fish and prawn balls for prawns and fish.

Yee Foo Mee

Restaurant Style

4 dessertspoons oil
2 cloves garlic, pounded
   finely
1 large onion, sliced finely
¼ kati (5¼ oz, 150 g) chicken,
   sliced finely
¼ kati (5¼ oz, 150 g) prawns
2½ cups (600 ml) chicken
   stock
Salt and pepper to taste
¼ kati (5¼ oz, 150 g) green
   vegetables, cut into pieces
10 Chinese mushrooms,
   soaked and sliced
One round yee foo mee (crisp
   fried noodles), scalded
   with boiling water and
   drained
A slice or two fresh ginger

Garnishing:
1 cup crab meat
Omelette, shredded finely
Coriander leaves

Put oil in pan. Add garlic and fry till brown. Add sliced onions.

Now add chicken and fry a little. Add prawns.

Add stock, pepper and salt and simmer.

Add vegetables. Leave to cook, then add the sliced mushrooms.

Add mee. Stir quickly. There must be sufficient stock to make a rather moist dish.

To serve, place mee on platter and decorate with crab meat, omelette and coriander leaves.

Note:
Use vegetables like kalian (kale) or chye-sim (mustard greens) or shredded cabbage.

Basic Chinese Soups

Any of these meat:
½ lb (225 g) chicken, cut into
   small pieces
½ lb (225 g) pork, cut into
   small pieces
½ lb (225 g) pork and crab
   balls
½ lb (225 g) fish (ikan kurau,
   threadfin), cut in pieces
½ lb (225 g) fish balls and
   prawn balls
½ lb (225 g) fish and prawn,
   finely minced, mixed and
   made into balls

2 cloves garlic, minced
2 - 3 slices ginger (optional)
3 - 4 cups water or stock
¼ - ½ seasoning cube if water
   is used
Salt and pepper to taste
3 dessertspoon oil

Garnishing:
4 garlic, minced and fried
   golden brown
Coriander leaves

Vegetables:
**With chicken or pork – use
   cauliflower, green peas,
   mushrooms (dry or tinned)
   shredded bamboo shoot,
   shredded yam beans
   – a little of each or what
   you fancy to make 2 cups**

**With pork and crab balls, fish
   and prawns – use cabbage
   (round or long) or any green
   leafy vegetable like pak
   choy**

Method for chicken and pork:
Heat oil in deep pan. Brown garlic, fry chicken or pork a little, adding salt and pepper. Add 4 cups of water and ginger and simmer till chicken is cooked. Add vegetables and chicken broth cube, and cook till vegetables reach degree of softness you like. Garnish with brown garlic and coriander leaves.

Method for fish & prawn, or pork & crab balls:
Heat oil in deep pan and brown garlic. Add water or stock to browned garlic and, when it boils, add the balls. When they float, add the vegetable, salt, pepper, ginger. Garnish with browned garlic and coriander leaves.

Method for fish:
Add vegetables to stock and, when nearly cooked, add pieces of fish.

Corn Soup

2 dessertspoons oil
1 clove garlic, minced
½ chicken (½ lb, 225 g)
1 dessertspoon salt
Pepper to taste
3 - 4 cups water
1 small tin cream-style sweet
  corn
Coriander leaves
1 dessertspoon finely sliced
  onions, fried till golden
  brown
½ cup cooked crab meat
  (optional)

Heat oil in pan. Brown garlic. Add chicken and fry for 5 minutes. Add 1 dessertspoon salt and a dash of pepper, and then water. Allow to simmer for ½ hour.

Remove chicken, cool and remove meat. Dice it and put aside for use later. Put chicken bones back into stock and allow to simmer for 30 minutes. Add the corn and add more water, and salt, if necessary.

Before serving, remove bones and add the diced chicken. Garnish individual bowls of soup with coriander leaves, fried onions and crab meat.

Pork, Crab & Prawn Ball Soup

½ kati (10½ oz, 300 g) lean
  pork, minced
1 teacup cooked crab meat
½ kati (10½ oz, 300 g) prawns,
  chopped
1 teaspoon flour
Salt and pepper
1 egg
3 dessertspoons oil
3 cloves garlic, pounded
3 teacups pork or chicken
  stock, if available
1½ teacups shredded
  bamboo shoot which has
  been previously boiled
1 teacup shredded
  bangkwang (yambean)
Coriander leaves
Fried pounded garlic

Mix the minced pork, crab meat and prawns in a bowl, add a teaspoon of flour, pepper, salt and an egg. Mix well with fingers and form into small balls and put aside for use later.

Put oil in deep pan, fry the garlic till golden brown. Add stock or water and salt. When boiling add shredded bamboo shoot and bangkwang and allow to cook for about 30 minutes. Drop the pork, crab and prawn balls one by one into pan, and allow to simmer till cooked.

To serve, place soup in deep dish and sprinkle on top coriander leaves and pounded garlic which has been fried till nice and brown.

Tauhu Puteh Soup

Soya Bean Curd Soup

3 dessertspoons oil
2 cloves garlic, finely minced
¼ lb (115 g) fresh medium-
    sized prawns, shelled,
    cleaned and halved
2½ cups water or stock from
    prawn shells or pork
    bones
4 squares soft type white
    tauhu (bean curd), or
    1 small round piece,
    cut into ½ in (1¼ cm) cubes
Salt and pepper to taste
¼ lb (115 g) ikan kurau
    (threadfin), coarsely diced
1 dessertspoon chopped local
    green celery
1 dessertspoon chopped
    spring onions

Heat oil in deep pan and brown garlic. Add prawns, fry a little and add water or stock. When boiling add bean curd pieces, salt and pepper, and allow to simmer for 20 minutes or more. Add fish and, after ten minutes, add chopped celery and spring onions and serve.

For variety:
For a pepper hot soup use, instead of garlic, a paste made from:
6 small onions
1 teaspoon white peppercorns
½ teaspoon blachan

If you use water add a small bouillon cube to improve taste.

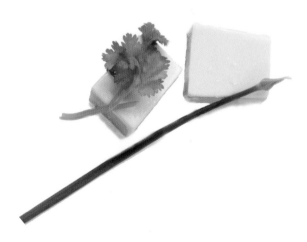

Fish Broth

1 level teacup rice
4 - 5 teacups water
1 dessertspoon sliced onions
  (small ones)
1 lb (450 g) fish (ikan kurau,
  threadfin), skin removed,
  diced
2 thin slices fresh ginger,
  finely shredded
1 teaspoon of seasoning
  powder
2 dessertspoons soya sauce
1 dessertspoon boiling oil
Salt and pepper to taste

Garnishing:
4 dessertspoons finely sliced
  small onions, fried golden
  brown
4 dessertspoons green celery,
  finely chopped
4 dessertspoons spring
  onion, finely chopped
Coriander leaves

Wash rice, add water and sliced onions and cook in a deep pan on medium heat till rice swells and begins to break. Do not stir, but add boiling water if necessary, and when rice has been broken up well, stir, adding more water to make the consistency you like.

In a dish, mix the diced fish, shredded ginger, seasoning powder, soy sauce and boiling oil. Add to the boiling broth, stirring well, adding salt and pepper.

Boil for five minutes and serve in bowls, garnishing top with fried onions, celery, spring onions and coriander leaves.

Note:
For those who like it hot, light soy sauce with finely sliced chillies goes well with this broth. Serve the condiment in separate dish.

For variety:
For Chicken Broth, substitute 1 ½ lb (750 g) chicken for the fish.

Boil chicken meat in water first for ½ hour. Remove chicken, cool, remove meat and put bones back into stock. Add rice, following above recipe.

Dice chicken meat, mixing it with ginger, seasoning powder etc, before adding to broth before serving.

Fish Ball Soup

1 kati (21 oz, 600 g) fish,
tenggiri (mackerel) or
parang (wolf herring)
Salt and pepper to taste

3 tablespoons cooking oil
4 cloves garlic, finely minced
or pounded
4 cups stock from pork bones
or chicken bones
2 oz (55 g) soohoon
(transparent vermicelli),
cut into 1½ in (3 cm) strips
and soaked in cold water
90g lettuce, shredded

Garnishing:
2 dessertspoons local green
celery, finely chopped
2 dessertspoons spring
onions, finely chopped
2 bundles coriander leaves
2 dessertspoons crisply fried
sliced onions
1 dessertspoon sliced red
chillies
2 dessertspoons tangchai
(pickled radish), (optional)

For making fish balls:
Remove fish from skin and bones, scraping it off with a spoon in thin layers. Chop fish a little on a wooden board or pass through mincer, then pound using pestle and mortar, adding water in which 1 teaspoon salt has been dissolved.

Add enough water to give fish a soft consistency that is handable. Add pepper and salt to taste and a little of the chopped celery and spring onions. (If you like a crispness in the fish balls, add a dessertspoon oil while pounding, and reduce the salted water).

Mix well with fingers. Scoop up pounded fish and throw the lump into the mortar several times to get it smooth. Form little balls, oiling your fingers slightly to prevent fish sticking to them, and drop them in a bowl of salted cold water. Put aside till required.

For variety:
Mix ½ kati (300 g) fish and ½ kati (300 g) prawns for the pounded mixture, or use ½ kati (300 g) fish for fish balls and 1 kati (600 g) prawns for prawn balls. Add to pounded mixture chopped bokgi (black wood fungus).

Method for Soup:
Put oil in deep pan and, when hot, fry garlic till golden brown. Add stock which has been strained and salt and pepper to taste. When boiling, add the fish balls and allow to simmer gently till fish balls are properly cooked. Add the soohoon and serve at once.

To serve, put shredded lettuce into dish and pour over it the fish ball soup.

Garnish top with chopped celery and spring onions, coriander leaves, fried onions and sliced chillies. If you care for tangchai add this too, washing it first.

Chilli, Ginger & Vinegar Sauce

4 red fresh chillies (seeded)
2 slices fresh ginger
3 dessertspoons vinegar
Salt to taste
Sugar to taste (optional)

Pound together chillies and ginger. Mix with vinegar and a little salt. Add a little sugar too, if you like a sweet sauce.

Sweet Sour Sauce with Garlic & Chilli Flavour

2 dessertspoons oil
2 cloves garlic, finely minced
1 teaspoon finely pounded
   fresh red chillies
1 large onion, cut into small
   wedges
1 large tomato, cut into small
   wedges
½ cup tomato sauce mixed
   with ¾ cup cold water
1 dessertspoon sugar to taste
1 dessertspoon vinegar
Salt to taste
1 dessertspoon cornflour

Heat oil in pan. Brown garlic and add pounded chillies. After a few seconds add onions and tomato. Fry a little, then add tomato sauce, sugar, vinegar and salt to taste. Allow to simmer for about five minutes and then stir in the cornflour made into a paste with a little water to thicken sauce.

This sauce can be used with fish or pork.

Malayan &
Indonesian Dishes

Beef Assam

1½ katis (2 lb, 900 g) beef, cut
  into small pieces
4 dessertspoons oil
1½ pints (3 cups) tamarind
  juice, from 2 teaspoons
  tamarind
Salt to taste
Sugar to taste

Pound together till fine:
6 dried chillies
5 buah keras (candlenuts)
15 small onions
1 teaspoon blachan
¼ teaspoon fresh turmeric
6 thick slices langkuas
  (galangal)

Put oil in pan and heat. Fry pounded ingredients till
brown.

Add in beef and fry for ten minutes, then tamarind
juice and boil.

Add salt and sugar to taste. Simmer till tender and
gravy thickens.

For variety:
Pork can be substituted for beef.

Curried Minced Beef

4 level dessertspoons
  vegetable oil
1 large onion, diced
2 cloves garlic, shredded
1 teaspoon shredded fresh
  ginger
2 level dessertspoons curry
  powder, mixed into a paste
  with a little water
1 lb (450 g) minced beef
1 large ripe tomato, diced
2 level dessertspoons tomato
  paste
1 teacup water
1 level dessertspoon salt, or
  to taste
4 hard-boiled eggs, halved

Heat oil in pan, fry onion, garlic and ginger till
slightly brown, add curry paste and a little water and
stir well.

When oil bubbles appear, add minced beef, stir well
and allow to cook a little. Then add tomato, tomato
paste, water and salt. Cover pan and allow to simmer
till meat is cooked and curry reaches the consistency
you want. This should be moist but not watery.

To serve, put curry in dish and place on top the halves
of hard-boiled eggs.

For variety:
Instead of minced beef, you can use minced pork,
lamb or chicken.

Beef in Soya Bean Sauce

½ kati (10½ oz, 300 g) good
  beef, cut into thin pieces
20 peppercorns, finely
  ground
Salt to taste
2 dessertspoons oil
2 tablespoons thick soya bean
  sauce
1 cup water (or more)
2 large onions, sliced
A small piece of cinnamon
2 cloves

Rub ground pepper and salt on meat and fry meat in
hot oil till a little brown.

Add sauce and water and allow to summer till meat
is soft.

Add onions and spices and cook till very little gravy
is left.

Note:
Sliced potato can be added.

Lamb with Soya Sauce, Onions & Tomato

3 dessertspoons oil
1 lb (450 g) lamb, cut into
  small pieces
1 level teaspoon white
  peppercorns, ground
Salt to taste
1 dessertspoon thick soy
  sauce
1 large onion, cut into wedges
2 large tomatoes, cut into
  wedges
½ in (1¼ cm) cinnamon
1½ cups water

Heat oil in frying pan. Fry lamb, which has been mixed
with pepper and salt, for about 15 minutes. Add soy
sauce, onions, tomato and cinnamon. Mix well. Then
add 1½ cups water, cover pan, and simmer on slow
fire till meat is tender and dry. Add more water if
meat requires more cooking.

This dish should be served dry.

Boiled Vegetable & Coconut Milk Sambal

½ kati (10½ oz, 300 g) of any
  one of the following
  vegetables, boiled:
  beansprouts
  shredded cabbage
  ladies' fingers

To make Sambal Blachan:
6 fresh red chillies, seeded
  and pounded with
  1 teaspoon roasted blachan

6 small onions, sliced fine
  and rubbed with salt and
  washed
Juice of 2 limes (limau kesturi)
¼ kati (5¼ oz, 150 g) steamed
  fresh prawns, halved, or
  2 tablespoons pounded
  dried prawns
1 teacup first squeeze
  coconut milk, boiled with
  1 teaspoon flour and a little
  salt

Mix together sambal blachan, sliced onions, salt, lime juice, prawns and coconut milk to suit your taste.

Arrange boiled vegetable in dish and pour the sambal mixture on top.

Chap Chye Lemak

4 dessertspoons oil

Pounded or ground:
6 chillies
2 teaspoons blachan
4 buah keras (candlenuts)
10 small onions

½ lb (225 g) fresh prawns, shelled and cleaned
1 oz (30 g) tauhu kee (fried beancurd skin), cut into 1½ in (4 cm) lengths and soak in warm water
1 oz (30 g) kim chiam (lily buds), remove stalk and soak in warm water
1 oz (30 g) dried mushrooms, remove stalks and soak in warm water
½ oz (15 g) bokgi (black wood fungus), remove stalks and soak in warm water
Salt to taste

¼ lb (115 g) cabbage, cut into small pieces
¼ lb (115 g) boiled bamboo shoot, sliced
3 pieces taukwa (firm soya bean cake), cut into small pieces and fried a little
½ oz (15 g) sohoon (mung bean vermicelli), cut into 1½ in (4 cm) lengths and soak in cold water
2 - 3 cups coconut milk from ¾ coconut (first squeeze, the rest second)

Heat oil in pan. Fry ground ingredients till well done and fragrant. Add prawns, fry a little and then add tauhu kee, kim chiam, dried mushrooms, bokgi, salt and enough second squeeze coconut milk to cover.

After 30 minutes add cabbage and bamboo shoot and continue to simmer till cabbage is cooked. Now add taukwa and sohoon and first squeeze coconut milk and simmer till gravy boils.

Note:
If you do not like a very rich dish, use less coconut.

Cabbage Sambal

3 dessertspoons vegetable oil
2 cloves garlic, sliced finely
10 small onions, sliced finely
4 large red chillies, seeded
  and sliced finely
2 chicken livers, boiled and
  sliced
2 chicken gizzards, boiled
  and sliced
Salt to taste
½ kati (10½ oz, 300 g)
  cabbage, sliced very finely
½ teaspoon blachan made
  into a paste with 2 dessertspoons thin tamarind juice
¾ teacup first squeeze
  milk from ½ coconut

Put oil in pan. Fry garlic till brown, add onions and chillies. Then add chicken liver, gizzard, salt, cabbage, blachan and tamarind paste. When cabbage is cooked, add coconut milk. When boiling remove pan from fire.

Gadoh-Gadoh

¼ kati (5¼ oz, 150 g) kangkong (water convolvulous), cut into short lengths and boiled
¼ kati (5¼ oz, 150 g) long beans, cut into 1 in (2½ cm) lengths
¼ kati (5¼ oz, 150 g) cabbage, shredded and scalded
5 cucumbers, cut into wedges
1 small bangkwang (yambean), cut into wedges
6 taukwa (hard soya bean cake), fried and cut into pieces
3 eggs, boiled and sliced
A few kroepoks (prawn crackers), fried and broken into small pieces
3 medium-sized potatoes, boiled and sliced
3 tempe (fermented soya bean cake), cut into pieces, mixed with salt and pepper and fried crisp
½ kati (10½ oz, 300 g) taugeh (beansprouts), cleaned and scalded

For gravy:
3 teacups coconut milk from ½ coconut
1½ teacups roasted peanuts, pounded quite finely
½ teacup tamarind juice
Gula melaka to taste
Salt to taste

Ground together:
20 – 24 fresh red chillies, half or all seeded
1 piece blachan (2 x 2 x 1 in, 5 x 5 x 1 cm)

Method I for making gravy:
Mix all the gravy ingredients and bring to boil. Allow to simmer for a few minutes, adding more salt, sugar and tamarind to suit your taste.

Method II for making gravy:
Add to gravy ingredients ½ cup small onions, ground finely.

Put about 3 dessertspoons oil in a deep pan, fry the ground small onions till soft, then the chilli and blachan paste. Add a little coconut milk and the peanuts, stirring till smooth. Add the tamarind juice, gula melaka, salt and rest of coconut milk. Simmer for a few minutes.

To serve:
Place vegetables etc, on platter and gravy in a deep dish. The kroepoks should be kept in a small bottle to keep crisp. Each person will help herself to what she likes from the vegetable platter and to as much gravy as she likes.

Indian Rojak

GRAVY:
3 - 4 dessertspoons cooking oil

Finely ground together:
16 dried chillies
25 small onions

⅓ kati (7 oz, 200 g) roasted
   peanuts, pounded finely
2 - 3 teacups tamarind juice
1½ teacups mashed boiled
   sweet potato
Salt to taste
Sugar to taste

TAPIOCA FRITTERS:
2½ teacups grated fresh
   tapioca
2 dessertspoons dried prawns
½ teaspoon turmeric powder
Salt to taste

Pounded coarsely together:
1 green chilli
1 red chilli
4 small onions

VEGETABLES ETC:
100 g taugeh (beansprouts),
   cleaned and scalded
1 bangkwang (yam bean),
   shredded
8 pieces taukwa (hard soya
   bean cakes), fried and
   thinly sliced
2 hard boiled eggs, sliced
2 cucumbers, shredded
2 potatoes, boiled in jackets,
   skinned, sliced, mixed with
   a little ground chilli and
   salt and fried
Prawns fritters (if desired)

To make gravy:
Put oil in pan and when hot, fry the ground chillies and onions. When cooked, add the pounded peanuts and some tamarind juice. Fry a little, then add mashed potato, a little at a time. Add salt and sugar to taste and as much tamarind juice as is required. Boil for about 15 minutes on slow fire, stirring to prevent burning.

For Tapioca Fritters:
Fry the pounded ingredients in a dessertspoon of oil
.
Mix the fried pounded ingredients with the other ingredients for the Tapioca Fritters. Form into a flat cakes and fry in hot oil, not deep, till brown, turning over when one side browns.

Remove the fritters from the oil, cool and slice them. Set aside.

To serve:
Arrange a little of each vegetable etc, on a plate, put a little gravy on top and add a few drops of soya sauce and vinegar.

Malay/Chinese Style Rojak

Pounded together:
10 fresh red chillies
2 teaspoons roasted blachan,

¾ cup roasted peanuts,
  pounded till grainy
1 cup tamarind sauce from
  1 dessertspoon tamarind,
  boiled
¼ - ½ cup gula melaka syrup
2 dessertspoons petis
  (heh koh, prawn paste)
Bunga kantan (phaeomeria),
  a few slices for flavouring
Juice for 2 limau kesturi,
  if desired
Salt to taste

Mix all ingredients, reducing or increasing tamarind and sugar to suit your taste.

Serve with small quantities of boiled kangkong, boiled taugeh (beansprouts), sliced fried taukwa (hard soya bean cake), and pineapple, cucumber and bangwang, all sliced.

Alternatively, mix vegetables etc. with sauce and serve on large platter.

Sauces for Malayan Salads

¼ cup chilli sauce 1
  (see page 192)
4 - 6 dessertspoons peanut
  butter
Sugar to taste
Salt to taste
Vinegar to taste
¾ cup cold boiled water

Mix the ingredients together to make the sauce.

For variety:
Add ¼ cup sweet mango chutney, chopped finely into the basic sauce.

In addition to the chopped mango chutney, add 3 dessertspoons roasted bijan (sesame seeds) which have been pounded a little.

These sauces can be served with slices of fried tauhu, cucumber, bangkwang, pineapple and scalded beansprouts.

Easy-to-make Rojak

Ingredients A:
4 cakes of taukwa (hard soya
  bean cake), fried whole
  till brown, and then cut into
  pieces
½ kati (10½ oz, 300 g) taugeh
  (beansprouts), cleaned and
  scalded
Cucumber, keep skin on,
  shredded
Bangkwang (yam bean),
  shredded
Pineapple, shredded
Tomato, sliced
4 hard boiled eggs, cut into
  wedges

Ingredients B:
4 heaping dessertspoons
  crunchy peanut butter
½ cup Chilli Sauce 2 (see
  page 193) or any good chilli
  sauce
2 dessertspoons thick gula
  melaka syrup
1 dessertspoon thick soya
  sauce
¾ cup cold boiled water
Sugar, salt and vinegar to suit
  your taste

Arrange Ingredients A in a platter.

Mix Ingredients B together to make the rojak sauce.

Dress Ingredients A with the sauce and serve.

127

Penang Pickle

¼ kati (5¼ oz, 150 g) long
  beans
¼ kati (5¼ oz, 150 g) French
  beans
¼ kati (5¼ oz, 150 g) ladies
  fingers
2 small carrots
6 large onions
3 radishes
1 large bitter gourd
¼ kati (5¼ oz, 150 g) cabbage
8 cucumbers

1½ teacups oil
1 large piece fresh turmeric,
  sliced very thinly

Ground together:
40 dried chillies, some seeded
15 slices langkwas (galangal)
1½ teacups small red onions
2 slices blachan, 2 x 2 x ½ in
  (5 x 5 x 1¼ cm) each

Sugar and salt to taste
1 teacup bijan (sesame
  seeds), cleaned, washed,
  drained and fried in dry
  pan till golden brown.
  Pound a little and put
  aside.

Cut all the vegetables into small pieces and scald in boiling vinegar to which a little salt has been added, one vegetable at a time. Drain in colander and put aside.

Put oil in pan. When hot fry sliced turmeric until brown. Remove and throw away.

Fry ground ingredients in hot till well cooked.

Add salt and sugar.

Add vegetables which have been scalded in vinegar. Stir well all the time for about 10 minutes.

Add fried and pounded bijan, stir well.

Remove to porcelain bowl to cool.

Notes from this edition:
Use 400 ml (1¾ teacups) of vinegar with 2 teaspoons of salt. After frying the ground ingredients till cooked and fragrant, add 5 tablespoons of sugar and salt to taste. You may wish to add another 2 tablespoons of sugar or more to taste after the vegetables have been added.

Simple Vegetable Pickle

4 cucumbers
1 cup small onions
1 cup of cauliflower
1 large carrot
6 fresh red chillies
6 fresh green chillies
2 tablespoons finely shredded fresh ginger

Ground together finely:
4 slices langkwas (galangal)
6 cloves garlic
1 in (2½ cm) very yellow
   turmeric

1 serai (lemongrass) bulb,
   1½ in (4 cm) from root, cut
   into four lengthwise
2 cups good white vinegar
8 tablespoons sugar, or to
   taste
2 dessertspoons salt, or to
   taste
4 dessertspoons vegetable oil

Cut each cucumber into quarters lengthwise, and remove pulp. Cut each piece into 1½ in (4 cm) lengths, and slit each piece three quarter way up from one end.

Skin and cut each onion into four, half way up from pointed end.

Cut the cauliflower into small pieces.

Skin and cut the carrot into 1½ in (4 cm) lengths, and each length halved and then coarsely sliced.

Slit the chillies in two up to stem.

Put all cut vegetables and the shredded ginger in a flat cane basket and dry in the sun all day.

Heat oil in pan. Fry ground ingredients till crisp and fragrant. Add serai, vinegar and salt and sugar to suit your taste. After this boils, pour it into a porcelain or Pyrex bowl to cool. Put in all vegetables, mix well and keep overnight.

Note:
This pickle should be made the day before you want to use it. It will keep for about three days. If kept in a refrigerator, it will keep longer.

Pineapple & Cucumber Sambal

8 fresh red chillies, all or a
few seeded
A piece of blachan, 2 x 1 x ¼ in
(5 x 2½ x ½ cm), roasted
4 dessertspoons good dried
prawns, well cleaned,
washed and soaked in
boiling water then drained
3 dessertspoons vinegar or
lime juice, optional
Salt to taste
Sugar to taste, optional
1 cucumber, cut into slices
3 thick slices ripe pineapple,
cut into pieces

Pound the chillies and roasted blachan till fine. Remove from mortar and then pound the dried prawns to break them up.

Mix the chillies and blachan paste, the pounded dried prawns, vinegar, salt and sugar with the cucumber and pineapple.

Serve with rice and curry or fried noodles.

Coconut Sambal

2 dessertspoons oil
6 small onions, finely sliced
2 oz (55 g) dried prawns,
cleaned, washed and finely
pounded
½ coconut, grated after
brown skin has been
removed
½ stalk serai (lemongrass),
finely sliced
2 red fresh chillies, finely
sliced, seeded first for a
mild sambal
Salt to taste

Heat oil in pan, fry onions till soft, then add the dried prawns. After a few minutes add coconut, serai and chillies, stirring all the time and using low heat. Add salt. Fry till golden brown.

Serve with rice and curry or with pulot (steamed with coconut milk and white beans).

Ikan Asam

Fish in Tamarind Juice and Curry Ingredients

4 dessertspoons vegetable oil

Ground together:
4 buah keras (candlenuts)
6 slices langkwas (galangal)
2 stalks serai (lemongrass),
   sliced
½ in (1¼ cm) fresh turmeric
8 large fresh red chillies,
   seeded
½ teacup small onions
1 small piece blachan
   (1 x 1 x ½ in, 2½ x 2½ x 1¼ cm)

2½ teacups thin tamarind
   juice from 2 teaspoons
   tamarind
½ kati (10½ oz, 300g) fish, cut
   into pieces
Salt to taste

Put oil in pan and when hot fry the ground ingredients till well cooked. Add tamarind juice and salt, and simmer till oil rises to the top. When boiling add fish and boil for another ten minutes or so.

For variety:
Use about ½ kati (10½ oz, 300g) large fresh prawns instead of fish. Do not shell the prawns for this curry.

Add 2 teacups fresh, ripe pineapple slices, or blimbing or tomatoes. These are to be added and allowed to cook before fish or prawns are put into the curry. Use less tamarind with pineapple, blimbing or tomatoes.

Curried Prawns

1 kati (21 oz, 600 g) very fresh
   large prawns.
1 teacup first squeeze milk
   from ½ coconut
Salt to taste

Ground together:
4 slices langkwas (galangal)
2 stalks serai (lemongrass),
   sliced
¼ in (½ cm) fresh turmeric
4 buah keras (candlenuts)
10 large red chillies, seeded
½ teacup small onions
½ teaspoon blachan

4 dessertspoons vegetable oil

Keep head and tails of prawns. Take off a little of the shell around middle and remove the dark thin streak down the back.

Mix prawns and all the other ingredients except the oil. Put oil in frying pan and when hot put in prawns, etc. Simmer, stirring occasionally, till prawns are properly cooked and dry.

For variety:
Instead of prawns, calf's liver, pork or chicken may be used.

Brinjal & Fish Curry

2-3 brinjals
4 tablespoons vegetable oil
1½ - 3 teacups tamarind juice
   from 2 teaspoons tamarind
Salt to taste
½ kati (10½ oz, 300 g) fresh
   fish, cut into pieces

Ground together:
5 buah keras (candlenuts)
6 slices langkwas (galangal)
2 stalks serai, sliced
1 dessertspoon peppercorns
2.5cm piece fresh turmeric
¾ teacup small onions
1 piece of blachan
   (1 x 1 x ½ in,
   2.5 x 2.5 x 1¼ cm)

Cut brinjals into 1½ in (4 cm) pieces and soak in water long before using. Wash and drain before using.

Put oil in pan and fry pounded ingredients till well cooked. Add a little tamarind juice and salt, and cook for about five minutes. When boiling, add the rest of the tamarind juice and allow to simmer.

When it is nearly cooked, add fish and allow to simmer till fish is properly cooked and oil rises to top.

For variety:
Use ½ - ¾ kati (10½ oz - 1 lb, 300 - 480 g) fresh prawns instead of fish.

If you like the flavour of salted fish, use good salted ikan kurau bones and a little of the salted fish itself. Add the bones and fish to the fried ingredients so that it can be properly cooked in the gravy before you add the brinjal.

Crab Curry

2 medium-sized crabs (about
2½ katis, 3⅓ lb, 1½ kg)
½ kati (10½ oz, 300 g) bittergourd
6 dessertspoons vegetable oil
2 cloves garlic, ground
½ teacup small onions,
ground

(A) Ground together:
4 tablespoons roasted
  ketumbar (coriander)
1 dessertspoon roasted jintan
  manis (anise)
1 dessertspoon roasted jintan
  puteh (cumin)
1 dessertspoon roasted
  peppercorns
½ in (1¼ cm) dry turmeric
4 buah keras (candlenuts)

4 - 5 teacups coconut milk
  from 1 coconut
3 thin slices ginger, finely
  shredded
6 dessertspoons grated
  coconut previously roasted
  in dry pan
Salt to taste
3 sprigs curry leaves

Boil the crabs and, when cool, remove all unwanted parts. Separate claws from body, removing as much of the shell as is necessary to allow meat to be picked out easily. Cut body into two or four pieces.

Cut the bitter gourd in two lengthwise, and remove seeds. Cut into thin slices and scald with boiling water. When cool, throw water away, squeeze all juice out of gourd to get rid of the bitter flavour.

Put oil in large pan, and when hot fry the ground garlic and onions till slightly brown. Add the ground ingredients A and stir well, adding a little coconut milk.

After about six minutes add ginger and ground coconut and more coconut milk. When boiling add the crab, bitter gourd, curry leaves, and salt, stirring well.

Add the rest of the coconut milk and allow to simmer until gravy thickens and reaches the consistency required.

Otak-Otak

6 dessertspoons grated
   coconut, fried till golden
   brown, slightly pounded
2½ dessertspoons roasted
   ketumbar, ground
   separately

Finely ground together:
3 stalks serai sliced
6 buah keras
¼ in (½ cm) piece dry
   turmeric
8 dried chillies, seeded
2 cloves garlic
10 small onions

¾ teacup first squeeze
   coconut milk from
   ¾ coconut
Salt to taste
½ kati (10½ oz, 300g) ikan
   kurau (threadfin), debone,
   cut into thin pieces or ½
   kati (10½ oz, 300g) fresh
   medium-sized prawns,
   shelled and cleaned
1 teaspoon daun kesum
   (laksa leaves) sliced very
   finely
Pieces of banana leaves,
   softened by steaming or
   boiled in water for a few
   minutes
Sharpened ribs of coconut
   leaves or toothpicks

Boil all ground ingredients with coconut milk and salt till thick enough to set. Remove from fire and when cool add uncooked fish or prawns. Add the chopped kesum leaves.

Place a little of the mixture in a piece of banana leaf, fold the two sides over each other and secure the ends with toothpicks. Make as many bundles of otak-otak as you can.

Grill them over a slow charcoal fire for about fifteen minutes, turning bundles when necessary.

Fish Moolie

1½ lb (680 g) red fish or 6
  slices ikan kurau (threadfin)
4 dessertspoons oil
2 large onions, coarsely
  sliced
4 thick slices ginger, cut into
  coarse strips

Pounded together:
1 stalk serai (lemongrass)
3 slices langkuas (galangal)
4 buah keras (candlenuts)
Small piece fresh turmeric

3 teacups coconut milk
  (1 cup first squeeze, rest
  second) from ¾ coconut
Vinegar to taste
Sugar to taste
Salt to taste
Flour for thickening

Trimmings:
Fried onions
Fried finely sliced garlic
  (optional)
Fried fresh ginger, sliced in
  long fine strips
Sliced green and red chillies,
  seeded if you like

Wash, drain and fry fish till golden brown.

Fry in oil the sliced onions and ginger till soft but not brown. Add pounded ingredients and fry till properly cooked.

Add second squeeze coconut milk and keep fire low. Add the fried fish and then the first squeeze coconut milk with vinegar, sugar and salt to taste.

Thicken with flour. Cook on gentle flame till gravy reaches consistency required.

Put in large patter and decorate with trimmings.

Curried Prawns with Cashew Nuts

3 dessertspoons vegetable oil
2 large onions
1 teaspoon shredded fresh
  ginger
4 cloves garlic, shredded

Make a paste with a little water:
½ teaspoon turmeric powder
½ teaspoon chilli powder

2½ lb (1.1 kg) fresh prawns,
  shelled, deveined and
  cleaned
2 large red tomatoes, cut into
  wedges
3 dessertspoons tomato paste
1 cup undiluted evaporated
  milk mixed with 3 tablespoons lemon juice to sour it
6 oz (170 g) button mushrooms,
  coarsely sliced
1 cup water
Salt to taste
4 oz (115 g) roasted cashew nuts

Heat oil in pan. Put in onions, ginger and garlic and fry till slightly golden. Add turmeric and chilli powder paste. Add prawns and fry until well cooked. Add tomato, tomato paste, milk, mushrooms, water and salt to taste.

Cook on slow heat till required consistency in gravy is reached, adding more water if necessary. Before serving mix in the roasted cashew nuts.

Garnish dish with sprigs of parsley or pickled green chillies.

Note:
Use more chilli powder if you want a hotter curry.

Note from this edition:
You may use buttermilk in place of evaporated milk with lime juice.

Salted Fish Roe Sambal

1 fish roe (2 sides) fried in two
  pieces, not too crisp
2 dessertspoons finely sliced
  small onions, washed in
  salt water and squeezed dry
2 fresh red or green chillies,
  seeded, sliced
Juice from two limes, or to
  taste

Mash the fried fish roe and mix with sliced onions, chillies and lime juice.

Sambal Goreng (1)

4 dessertspoons oil

Ground together:
2 stalks serai (lemongrass),
   sliced
4 buah keras (candlenut)
4 slices langkuas (galangal)
10 large red chillies or
   6 fresh and 6 dried chillies
½ teacup small onions
½ teaspoon blachan

1 kati (21 oz, 600 g) prawns,
   shelled and cleaned
Salt to taste
1 teacup thick coconut milk
   from ½ coconut
½ teacup thin tamarind juice

Put oil in pan and when hot fry ground ingredients till well cooked. Add prawns and salt, stir and put in coconut milk and tamarind juice. Taste to see that there is enough salt and tamarind, adjust as desired. Cook on slow fire till thick and oil rises to the top.

Variation:
Leave out tamarind juice and add 10 blimbings, sliced into thin round pieces or cut into two.

Leave out tamarind juice and add 2 tomatoes cut into small wedges.

To make Sardine Sambal Goreng, use sardines instead of fresh prawns.

Sambal Goreng (2)

4 dessertspoons oil

Ground together:
10 dry chillies, seeded
4 buah keras (candlenuts)
1 teaspoon blachan
½ teacup small onions

Salt to taste
1 teacup first squeeze
   coconut milk from
   ½ coconut
½ teacup thin tamarind juice
½ kati (10½ oz, 300 g) prawns,
   shelled, cleaned and fried
or 300g fish (parang, kurau or
   tenggiri) fried, not too crisp

Put oil in pan and when hot fry ground ingredients till well cooked. Add salt, coconut milk and tamarind juice and when boiling add prawns or fish. Allow to simmer till gravy is thick and oil rises to the top.

Note:
Ikan parang is wolf herring, kurau is threadfin and tenggiri is mackerel.

Variation:
To make Sardine Sambal Goreng, use sardines instead of fresh prawns.

Sambal Goreng (3)

4 dessertspoons oil

Sliced finely:
¾ teacup onions
12 fresh red chillies, seeded

Ground together:
4 slices langkuas (galangal)
2 stalks serai (lemongrass)
1 teaspoon blachan
4 buah keras (candlenuts)

1 teacup thick coconut milk
   from ½ coconut
Salt to taste
1 kati (21 oz, 600 g) prawns,
   shelled and cleaned, fried
   with a little salt

Put oil in pan, fry sliced onions and chillies till soft. Add ground ingredients and fry till well cooked.

Add coconut milk and salt to taste. When boiling, add prawns and allow to simmer till gravy reaches the consistency desired.

For variety:
A little tamarind juice may be added to gravy if desired.

Use chicken livers (previously boiled and sliced) instead of prawns.

Prawn Sambal with Serai

4 dessertspoons oil
2 dessertspoons finely sliced
   small onions

Pound or grind to a paste:
4 red fresh chillies
1 buah keras
1 slice langkuas
½ teaspoon blachan

4 stalks serai (lemongrass),
   remove hard outer layers
   and slice very finely using
   about 1 in (2½ cm) from
   root
1 lb (450 g) fresh prawns,
   shelled and cleaned
1 teacup coconut milk from
   ½ coconut
4 red and green fresh chillies,
   seeded and finely sliced

Heat oil in pan, add onions and fry till soft. Add in ground ingredients and sliced serai. When well done add prawns and salt.

Fry a little and then add coconut milk. Allow to simmer till oil rises to the top. Add sliced chillies before removing from fire.

Soto Ayam

A Savoury Chicken Soup

1 cup macaroni (elbows or
  small pieces)
3 dessertspoons vegetable oil

Ground finely together:
1½ teaspoons white
  peppercorns
4 thin slices langkwas
  (galangal)
4 buah keras (candlenuts)
1 level dessertspoon
  coriander (ketumbar)
10 small onions

1 serai (lemongrass) bulb,
  2 in (5 cm) from root,
  bruised a little, to be used
  whole
6 cups water
Salt to taste
3 stalks of local celery
1 small chicken, cleaned and
  cut into 4 pieces

Garnishing:
Browned onions
Chopped celery
Chopped spring onions,
  if desired

Boil macaroni in salted water, wash in cold water and drain. Set aside.

Heat oil in deep pan and fry the ground ingredients till crisp and fragrant, stirring all the time. Add lemongrass stalk, water, salt and celery stalks. When boiling put in the chicken and allow to simmer till chicken is cooked.

Remove chicken on to plate. When cool, remove meat from bones and dice chicken. Put diced chicken back into the pan and as much of the macaroni as you require, and more water, if necessary.

Serve in small bowls and garnish with browned onions and chopped celery.

For variety:
You can use cut up ketupat (rice cakes) instead of the macaroni. You may also add softened soohoon (transparent vermicelli) to this soup instead.

Chicken Soup

2 dessertspoons vegetable
oil or 1 spoon oil and 1
spoon of butter
1 clove garlic, finely minced
1 chicken, cut into pieces
2 cloves, small piece of
cinnamon, piece of nutmeg
the size of a green pea, tied
up in a small piece of
muslin
Salt to taste
2 large onions
2 medium sized potatoes
2 tomatoes
2 carrots, cut into small
pieces
2 stalks local green celery,
coarsely chopped
10 peppercorns
2 dessertspoons finely sliced
onions, fried golden brown
for garnishing

Heat oil in deep pan. Brown garlic, add chicken and fry for 3 minutes. Add 1½ cups water, bag of spices and salt and boil till chicken is tender. Then add all other ingredients, adding more water, if necessary, and simmer till vegetables are cooked.

Serve in large dish or individual cups, garnishing with fried onions.

Notes:
Substitute for vegetables 20 medium sized dried mushrooms, previously soaked in boiling water and from which stalks have been removed, whole or cut into quarters.

If vegetables are used you can substitute beef for chicken.

Basic Curry

4 dessertspoons vegetable oil
2 dessertspoons chopped
onions
A slice of ginger, chopped
finely
3 dessertspoons curry powder
made into a paste with a
little water
1 lb (450 g) beef or chicken,
cut into small pieces
2 tomatoes, cut into small
pieces, optional
½ lb (225 g) potatoes, cut into
small pieces
2 teacups milk

Place oil in deep pan, fry onions till golden brown, add ginger; then add curry paste, stirring for a few seconds.

Add the meat, mix well, fry for about ten minutes. Add tomatoes and salt. Cover pan and cook till meat is tender.

Add potatoes and milk and cook till potatoes are done and gravy reaches consistency required.

Chicken Curry with Jintan Puteh Flavour

4 dessertspoons vegetable oil
2 cloves garlic, finely sliced
1 teaspoon shredded ginger
3 dessertspoons finely sliced
  small onions

Ground finely together:
16 dried chillies
  (all seeded for a mild curry)
1 level dessertspoon
  ketumbar (coriander)
2½ level dessertspoons
  jintan puteh (cumin)
1 in (2½ cm) piece dried
  turmeric

Coconut milk (½ cup first
  squeeze, and 2 cups second)
  from ½ grated coconut
1 chicken
Salt to taste
1 in (2½ cm) piece cinnamon
  stick
6 cardamons
6 cloves

Heat oil in pan, brown garlic, onions and ginger. Add ground curry paste and a little of the second squeeze of coconut milk. When fragrant and oil bubbles appear, add chicken, salt and the whole spices, stirring well. Cover pan and allow to cook on medium heat for 15 minutes, stirring once in a while to prevent burning.

Then add the second squeeze of coconut milk and simmer till chicken is tender. Now add first squeeze of coconut milk, and leave to simmer in open pan till oil rises to the top.

Note:
If you like a lot of gravy, make more of the second squeeze of coconut milk.

Hot Chilli Curry (1)

4 dessertspoons vegetable oil
30 dried red chillies, each cut
   into 3 pieces, lengthwise
25 small onions, finely sliced
1 chicken, cut into pieces
Salt to taste

Ground to a paste:
4 cloves
1 small piece cinnamon,
1 teaspoon jintan manis
   (anise)

1 cup first squeeze, 1 cup
   second squeeze coconut
   milk from ½ coconut

Heat pan, put in oil and fry chillies. Add onions and, when half cooked, add chicken and stir well. Add salt and then the ground ingredients and second squeeze coconut milk.

Cook on steady fire till chicken is about cooked. Add first squeeze milk and allow to simmer till gravy is thick.

Note:
Seed chillies if you prefer a mild curry.

Hot Chilli Curry (2)

4 dessertspoon vegetable oil
25 onions, finely sliced
15 green chillies, sliced

Ground to a fine paste:
3 tablespoons ketumber
   (coriander)
1 teaspoon jintan manis
   (anise)
1 teaspoon peppercorns
1 teaspoon kas-kas
   (poppy seeds)
Turmeric, size of 2 peas
1 in (2½ cm) cinnamon

1 chicken, cut into pieces
Salt to taste
1 cup first squeeze, 2 cups
   second squeeze coconut
   milk from 1 coconut
2 dessertspoons lime juice

Heat oil in pan. Add onions and green chillies. When half cooked, add ground ingredients and fry till well done. Put in chicken, stir well. Add salt and cover for 10 minutes.

Add second squeeze of milk and cook till chicken is soft. Add first squeeze of milk and allow to simmer till oil rises to top and gravy has reached consistency required.

Remove pan from fire and add lime juice while curry is still hot.

Note:
Seed chillies if you prefer a mild curry.

Chicken Curry

1 chicken, cut into pieces
3 - 4 teacups coconut milk
from 1 coconut (1 cup first
squeeze, 2 cups second)
Salt

(A) Ground together:
2 dessertspoons ketumbar
1 dessertspoon jintan manis
1 dessertspoons jintan puteh
12 dried chillies, seeded
½ in (1¼ cm) dry turmeric

(B) Ground together:
3 buah keras (candlenuts)
1 serai (lemongrass) stalk,
sliced
3 slices langkuas (galangal)
16 small onions
2 cloves garlic

Boil chicken in 2 cups second squeeze coconut milk, adding salt, till it is tender and milk becomes oil. Fry ground ingredients A and after about ten minutes add ground ingredients B.

Fry well and, when cooked, add the one cup of first squeeze coconut milk. Simmer till gravy becomes thick.

Note:
You can use beef, lamb or pork instead of chicken.

Kiam Chye & Chicken Curry

½ kati (10½ oz, 300g) kiam
chye (salted vegetable)
4 dessertspoons oil

Ground together:
4 buah keras (candlenuts)
6 slices langkuas (galangal)
½ in (1¼ cm) fresh tumeric
10 fresh red chillies, seeded
½ teaspoon blachan
12 small onions

½ kati (10½ oz, 300g) chicken,
cut into pieces
Salt to taste
2½ cups coconut milk (½ cup
first squeeze, rest second)
from ½ coconut
½ cup tamarind juice

Cut kiam chye into pieces and soak in water. Before using vegetable squeeze juice out and wash thoroughly so it will not be too salty.

Put oil in pan. Fry ground ingredients till well cooked. Add chicken and salt and fry for about 15 minutes. Add kiam chye and 2 cups second squeeze coconut milk and allow to simmer for an hour or so.

Add the rest of the coconut milk and some tamarind juice to suit your taste. Simmer till gravy reaches right consistency.

Variation:
Use pork, if you prefer it to chicken.

Chicken & Bamboo Shoot Curry

4 tablespoons vegetable oil
½ cup small red onions,
  finely sliced

Ground to a smooth paste:
2 dessertspoons ketumbar
  (coriander)
4 buah keras (candlenuts)
4 thin slices langkwas
  (galangal)
10 dried chillies
1 teaspoon blachan

1½ cups coconut milk from
  ¾ coconut (½ cup first
  squeeze, 1½ cups second
  squeeze)
½ chicken, cut into pieces
1 dessertspoon salt
2 cups sliced bamboo shoot,
  previously boiled for about
  3 hours

Heat oil in deep saucepan and fry the sliced onions till soft. Then add the ground ingredients, fry for 10 minutes till fragrant, adding two tablespoons of the second squeeze coconut milk. Add the chicken and a dessertspoon salt, stir well and cook for 15 minutes.

Now add the second squeeze of coconut milk and bamboo shoot, cover pan and simmer till chicken is tender. Then add the first squeeze coconut milk and continue to simmering till oil rises to the top. Taste and add more salt if desired.

Country Captain (1)

Curry Capitan

Ground together:
2 cloves garlic
1 teaspoon peppercorns
½ in (1¼ cm) piece dry turmeric

1 chicken, cut into pieces
1½ teacups first squeeze coconut milk from ¾ coconut
Salt to taste
½ teacup small onions, sliced finely, fried brown
2 cloves garlic, sliced finely, fried brown
Juice of 1 lime

This is a dry curry and is like spiced fried chicken.

Rub ground ingredients over the chicken, add all the coconut milk and salt, and let this simmer gently, till chicken is tender and dry. Fry sliced onions and garlic in oil and add to the chicken. Season with lime juice.

Country Captain (2)

Use same ingredients as for Dry Curry (page 204), only substituting pepper for chillies.

Use the method for Country Captain (1).

You can also use ordinary curry powder with chilli flavour.

Dried Curried Chicken

1 chicken, cut into pieces

Ground together:
10 (or more) dry red chillies
5 buah keras (candlenuts)
½ teacup small onions
½ teaspoon blachan

Salt to taste
1 teacup first squeeze
   milk from ½ coconut
4 dessertspoons vegetable oil

Mix chicken with ground ingredients, salt and coconut milk. Leave to stand for about 15 minutes. Heat oil in frying pan, and pour in chicken, etc, and cook over a slow fire, covering pan at first.

When chicken is tender, remove cover and stir till ingredients turn slightly brown.

Roast Chicken with Satay Flavour

2 dessertspoons oil

Finely ground together:
2 fresh chillies, seeded
1 dessertspoon ketumbar
   (coriander)
1½ teaspoons jintan puteh
   (cumin)
½ teaspoon jintan manis
   (anise)
½ in (1¼ cm) serai (lemongrass)
1 slice langkwas (galangal)
2 buah keras (candlenut)
Piece of turmeric, size of
   green pea
8 small onions
½ teaspoon sugar

Salt
1¼ cup coconut milk from
   ¼ coconut
1 dessertspoon tamarind
Juice from 1 teaspoon
   tamarind
1 chicken

Heat oil in pan and fry ground ingredients till fragrant, for about 5 minutes, stirring to prevent burning. Add 1 teaspoon salt. Remove pan from heat and cool.

Mix the coconut milk and tamarind juice.

Now rub inside and outside of the chicken with about ¾ dessertspoon salt and fried ingredients. Place chicken in roasting pan or deep pie dish, pour over gently, the coconut milk and tamarind mixture. Roast in moderate oven for about 1½ hours or till done, basting once in a while. Chicken should be nicely browned and gravy thick.

To serve, cut chicken into small pieces, place in large flat platter and pour the thick gravy over it.

Chicken Pot Roast

1 small chicken
Salt to taste

Ground together:
½ teaspoon peppercorns
A small piece of cinnamon
2 cloves
A very small piece of nutmeg
  about the size of 2 pepper
  corns

3 dessertspoons butter
2 dessertspoons good thick
  soya bean sauce
1 teacup water

Rub ground ingredients and salt inside and outside chicken. Fry in hot butter in deep pan for about ten minutes, turning it from time to time, without breaking the skin.

Add sauce and water, and more salt, if necessary. Cover pan and allow to simmer till chicken is cooked and there is very little gravy.

Duck Pot Roast

1 duck, whole
2 tablespoons roasted
  ketumbar (coriander),
  finely pounded
1 teaspoon peppercorns,
  finely pounded
1 dessertspoon sugar
Salt to taste
2 - 4 tablespoons thick soya
  bean sauce
3 tablespoons vegetable oil
½ teaspoon small onions,
  pounded
2 teacups water
Cinnamon for flavouring
Cloves for flavouring

Rub over the duck the ground ketumbar and pepper, a little sugar, salt and soya bean sauce.

Put oil in pan and fry the onions till well cooked. Add the duck and fry till a little brown, turning it round and round. Add water and spices and simmer till duck is cooked and very little gravy is left.

Laksa Siam

FOR GRAVY:

2 tablespoons thick soya bean
   sauce
1 in (2½ cm) cube gula melaka
Salt
1½ kati (2 lb, 900 g) fresh
   prawns, shelled and
   cleaned
12 small onions, roasted in
   skins
4 cloves garlic, roasted in
   skins
1½ teacups roasted peanuts,
   pounded
3 - 4 teacups cold water
Lime juice from two limes
   (limau nipis), to taste
1 dessertspoon chilli powder
4 cloves garlic, sliced and
   fried till golden brown
3 dessertspoons freshly
   made coconut oil (see method)

¾ kati (1 lb, 480 g) coarse
   beehoon (rice vermicelli)
½ kati (10½ oz, 300 g)
   kangkong
   (water convolvulous)
½ kati (10½ oz, 300 g) kachang
   botol (four-angled bean),
   sliced and fried
20 - 30 dried chillies, fried
   whole in oil, till they are
   crisp, but not burnt
2 teacups shredded half-ripe
   papaya
2 teacups jantong pisang
   (banana flower), if desired,
   boiled and separated into
   sections

For this dish you must have freshly made coconut oil.
The milk from one large coconut boiled down to oil
will give the required amount. Add 2 teacups water
to grated coconut, squeeze out the milk and place in
refrigerator to cool. Skim off the fat and boil slowly in
kwali (wok) till oil forms.

Add to 2 cups of water the soya bean sauce, gula
melaka and salt. Bring to the boil and then add
prawns. Simmer till prawns are well cooked.

Wash grinding stone well and grind to a paste the
roasted onions and garlic after removing the skin.
Remove paste to a plate.

Grind the cooked prawns to a smooth paste.

Add onion paste to the gravy in the pan, mix in the
ground prawns and pounded peanuts. When well
mixed, gradually add the cold boiled water, lime juice
and salt to taste. Add more sugar if necessary. Pour
gravy into a deep dish.

Heat oil in frying pan, fry the chilli powder a little and
pour this over the gravy, adding the fried garlic. Put
gravy aside for use later, without heating.

Scald coarse beehoon well with boiling water twice,
wash in cold water and drain. When dry, place in a
large platter.

Slice and fry kangong in freshly made coconut oil and
a little salt.

Sprinkle a little salt in the shredded half-ripe papaya
and allow to stand for a little while to soften it. Then
add a little water and squeeze out all the juice.
Arrange vegetables in a large platter.

To serve, put a small portion of beehoon in a soup
plate, pour over it as much gravy as you like and a
little of each vegetable. Crush dried chillies to use as
condiment.

Laksa

FOR GRAVY:
½ teacup vegetable oil
2 dessertspoons roasted
   ketumbar (coriander),
   ground separately

Ground together:
3 stalks serai (lemongrass),
   sliced
½ teacup (about) langkwas
6 buah keras (candlenuts)
12 – 14 dried chillies, seeded
   ½ in (1¼ cm) turmeric
A slice of blachan (2 x 2 x ½ in,
   5 x 5 x 1¼ cm)
1 teacup small onions

1 kati (21 oz, 600 g) fresh
   prawns, shelled and
   cleaned
Salt to taste
7 to 8 teacups coconut milk
   (2 cups first squeeze, rest
   second) from 1½ coconuts
Very small fish balls made
   from ½ kati (10½ oz, 300 g)
   tenggiri (mackeral) or
   parang (wolf herring)

FOR NOODLES:
12 tahils (1 lb, 480 g) coarse
   beehoon (rice vermicelli)
½ kati (10½ oz, 300 g) taugeh
   (beansprouts), cleaned,
   scalded and drained

FOR GARNISHING:
1 cucumber, skinned, cored
   and shredded
Daun kesom (laksa leaves),
   finely shredded
10 fresh chillies, finely
   pounded

Put oil in deep pan and, when hot, add ground ingredients, including coriander, and fry until well cooked and oil begins to separate from ingredients.

Add the prawns and a little salt. Fry for about five minutes and then add the 5 cups of second squeeze coconut milk.

When it boils, add the fish balls and when it is cooked, add the 2 cups of first squeeze coconut milk, adding more salt if necessary, and stirring gravy gently to prevent coconut milk curdling. Keep fire low. When gravy boils, remove pan from fire.

If gravy is cooked early, heat it before serving but do not let it boil again.

Wash coarse beehoon in cold water, removing all black specks. Then drain. Place beehoon in basin, pour over it boiling water and stir well. Drain in colander. Scald again and drain, if necessary, to soften it. To save time, beehoon can be boiled for a few minutes.

To serve, put a little taugeh and beehoon in a cup or soup plate. Pour over as much gravy as is required and garnish.

Note:
Chicken can be used instead of prawn and fish balls. Only steam the meat. Add whatever chicken stock there is from the steamed chicken to the gravy.

Malay Mee

Mee Rebus

2 lb (1 kg) beef, mutton or
   chicken
Local celery
Salt and pepper to taste
3 tablespoons vegetable oil

(A) Ground together:
24 dried chillies or less,
   seeded
5 buah keras (candlenut)
6 slices langkwas (galangal)
½ teacup small onions

3 dessertspoons ketumbar
   (coriander), ground
   separately
2 dessertspoons taucheo
   (soya bean paste), ground
   separately
1 teacup mashed cooked
   sweet potato
1½ kati (2 lb, 900 g) mee
   (yellow noodles), to be
   scalded when required
½ kati (10½ oz, 300 g)
   beansprouts, to be scalded
   when required

FOR GARNISHING:
Fried sliced onions
Thinly shredded omelette
Spring onions, finely chopped
Local celery, finely chopped
Kuchai (chives), finely chopped
Green and red chillies,
   finely sliced
6 taukwa (hard soya bean
   cake), fried and sliced finely
Lime juice
Chinese soya bean sauce
Vinegar

Boil the meat in one piece till well cooked, adding celery, salt and pepper. There should be about 5 teacups of stock. When cooked, remove meat from stock, dice and put aside, keeping it moist with a little stock. Keep rest of stock for use later.

Heat oil in deep pan. Fry combined ground ingredients (A). Add ground ketumbar and fry for a few minutes. Add ground taucheo, frying a little longer.

Add diced meat, mix well. Add stock and salt if necessary. Add mashed sweet potato to thicken gravy.

To serve, put in soup plate scalded mee and bean sprouts. Add gravy and diced meat. Garnish to taste.

Mee Siam (1)

5 teacups milk (2 cups first
    squeeze, rest second
    squeeze) from 2 coconuts

(A) Ground together:
40 dried chillies, seeded,
    ground
1½ teacups small onions
A piece of blachan (2 x 2 x ½ in,
    5 x 5 x 1¼ cm)

4 tablespoons taucheo,
    ground
1 teaspoon sugar, or to taste
Salt
1½ kati (2 lb, 900 g) taugeh
    (beansprouts), cleaned
1 kati (21 oz, 600 g) beehoon
    (rice vermicelli), scalded,
    washed under tap and
    drained
1½ kati (2 lb, 900 g) small
    prawns, shelled and cleaned
1 cup tamarind juice from
    2½ teaspoons tamarind
2 dessertspoons vegetable oil

FOR GARNISHING:
Seasoned prawns
4 eggs made into omelette
    and shredded or 4 hard
    boiled eggs, wedged
8 small pieces taukwa (hard
    soya bean cake) sliced
    finely and fried a little, but
    not crisp
¼ kati (5¼ oz, 150 g) kuchai
    (chives), cut into ½ in (1¼
    cm) lengths
Sliced red and green chillies
Limau kesturi (calamansi)
    cut into halves

Method for frying the beehoon:
Put in a large kwali the two cups of first squeeze
coconut milk and boil till it becomes oil. Add a little
more oil without removing the brown residue. Fry
ground ingredients (A) and, when cooked, add half
the amount of ground taucheo.

Fry well, add a teaspoonful of sugar and a little salt.
Remove a cupful of fried ingredients.

Now have a very big fire and add the taugeh and mix
well with the ingredients. Quickly push taugeh to the
side of kwali making a well, and place beehoon in the
liquid that will drain away from taugeh to the centre.
Add a little more salt and stir quickly. Mix in taugeh
and when thoroughly mixed, remove beehoon to a
large basin.

Method for preparing seasoned prawns:
Put in kwali a tablespoon of the fried ingredients and
fry prawns in it, adding a little more salt, if necessary.
When cooked, removed prawns from pan to a dish
for use as accompaniment.

Method for preparing gravy:
Put in kwali the rest of the fried ingredients and the
remaining 2 tablespoons of taucheo. Fry a little, then
add 3 teacups of the second squeeze coconut milk,
and the tamarind juice and salt to taste. Allow gravy
to simmer for a few minutes. Put into a deep dish.

To serve:
Put a little beehoon in plate, decorate top with
seasoned prawns and other garnishing and one or
two pieces of lime. Add as much gravy as you like.

Note:
If more gravy is required use more coconut milk.

Mee Siam (2)

Coconut oil made from
  2½ coconuts the day before,
  keeping the light brown
  residue (see page 155)
1 cup small red onions,
  ground
30 - 40 dried chillies, seeded,
  ground
1½ - 2 kati (2 - 2½ lb, 900 g - 1.2 kg)
  prawns, shelled, coarsely
  sliced
Salt to taste
15 - 20 pieces taukwa (hard
  soya bean cake), coarsely
  shredded

1¾ kati (2.2 lb, 1 kg) beehoon
  (rice vermicelli), scalded,
  washed under tap and
  drained
¾ kati (1 lb, 450 g) taugeh
  (beansprouts), cleaned
½ kati (10½ oz, 300 g) kuchai
  (chives), cut some from 2 in
  (5 cm) lengths from head for
  garnish, cut the rest into 1
  in (2½ cm) lengths to be
  cooked with beehoon

4 - 5 dessertspoons taucheo
  (soya bean paste), coarsely
  pounded

FOR GARNISHING:
Omelette, shredded finely
Red and green fresh chillies,
  seeded and sliced finely
2 bundles coriander leaves
1 cucumber, cored, shredded
12 limau kesturi (calamansi),
  cut into two
Kuchai (chives), cut into 2 in
  (5 cm) lengths (see above)

Method for making the dressing:
Heat 3 dessertspoons oil in kwali (wok), keeping the residue for later. Fry the ground onions and chilli for about 10 minutes or till it is cooked

Add prawns and salt, dry well and add the coconut oil residue. Keep on frying, stirring well.

Add taukwa, leave to simmer till taukwa is cooked, stirring to prevent burning.

Method for preparing the beehoon:
Put in large pan or kwali 3 - 4 dessertspoons of the dressing and about ⅓ of beehoon. When well mixed, make a well in centre add a handful of taugeh and a handful of kuchai and salt and cover with beehoon.

After about 7 - 10 minutes stir beehoon and when sufficiently cooked remove to a large bowl.

Repeat process till all the beehoon is used up.

Method for preparing taucheo:
Skim off a little oil from dressing and fry the pounded taucheo till it smells good. Add about 1½ teacups water and cook till it boils.

To serve:
Put prepared beehoon in large platter. Spread with dressing.

Decorate with omelette, sliced chillies and coriander leaves. Arrange around the edge of platter, the shredded cucumber, long strips of kuchai and limes.

Serve taucheo in separate dish.

Nasi Goreng (1)

Fried Rice

4 dessertspoons oil
4 fresh red chillies, seeded,
   pounded finely
6 - 8 small onions, pounded
   finely
3 oz (85 g) fresh prawns, diced
2 oz (55 g) ham, diced
1 oz (30 g) mushrooms, diced
2 oz (55 g) cooked pork or
   chicken breast, diced
6 teacups cold boiled rice,
   well broken up
Salt to taste
2 eggs, beaten
1 spring onion, chopped
   finely
2 celery stems, chopped
   finely

Put oil in pan and, when hot, fry pounded chillies and onions till well cooked.

Add prawns, ham, mushrooms and meat, then boiled rice. Stir well, adding salt to taste.

Add beaten eggs and stir till egg is cooked and rice is dry. Add chopped spring onions and celery.

Place in a large platter and serve.

Note:
Rice for Nasi Goreng must be cold. Therefore cook your rice long before you make this dish.

Nasi Goreng (2)

Fried Rice

3 dessertspoons oil
8 small onions, sliced very
   finely
4 red chillies, sliced very
   finely
2 oz (55 g) fresh prawns, diced
2 oz (55 g) cooked ham, diced
4 teacups cold boiled rice
Salt to taste
1 teaspoon soya sauce
2 eggs, beaten
1 tablespoon chopped spring
   onion
1 tablespoon chopped celery

Put oil in pan and when hot, fry sliced onions and chillies till soft. Add prawns and ham. Fry for a few minutes.

Add rice, mix well, adding salt and a little soya sauce to make it a little brown. Add beaten eggs and stir till egg is cooked and rice is dry.

Add chopped spring onions and celery. Place in a large platter and serve.

Pulot Panggang

Grilled Rice Rolls with Filling

1 kati (21 oz, 600 g) pulot
(glutinous rice), washed and
drained
2 teacups coconut milk from
1 coconut, remove brown
skin before grating
Salt to taste
2 dessertspoons vegetable oil
¼ kati (5¼ oz, 150 g) good
dried prawns, cleaned,
washed and pounded finely

Finely pounded together:
2 fresh red chillies
12 small onions
½ teaspoon peppercorns
3 buah keras (candlenuts)
1 level dessertspoon roasted
ketumbar (coriander)
½ teaspoon blachan

½ coconut, scraped after
brown skin has been
removed, fried in dry pan
till golden brown, and
pounded
1 teaspoon sugar
Pieces of banana leaves,
softened by steaming or
boiled in water for a few
minutes
Sharpened ribs of coconut
leaves or toothpicks

Mix the pulot with coconut milk and salt and steam till cooked, but not soft. Keep aside.

Put oil in pan. Fry the pounded prawns and when a little crisp, remove from pan.

Fry the finely pounded ingredients in the oil: when well cooked add pounded fried coconut, prawns, salt and sugar to taste.

Use banana leaves, which have been softened by steaming, to make rolls of pulots with prawns filling inside. Rolls can be about 3 in (7½cm) long, and 1 in (2½ cm) in circumference. Secure ends of rolls, with toothpicks. Roast these rolls over slow charcoal fire, turning them over when necessary, for about 20 - 30 minutes.

Note:
If fresh prawns are used instead of the dried ones, you will need ½ kati (10½ oz, 300 g), finely chopped.

Taukwa Sambal

4 dessertspoons oil

Ground together:
1 stalk serai (lemongrass),
    sliced
4 buah keras (candlenuts)
2 sliced langkwas (galangal)
8 fresh red chillies
12 small onions
2 teaspoons blachan

½ lb (225 g) fresh medium-
    sized prawns, shelled,
    cleaned and halved
Salt to taste
1½ cups coconut milk
    (½ cup first squeeze, rest
    second) from ½ coconut
6 taukwa (hard soya bean
    cake), cut into pieces

Heat oil in pan. Fry ground ingredients for about 10 minutes till fragrant. Then add prawns and a little salt. Add the second squeeze coconut milk. When this boils, add the taukwa and cook for 10 minutes.

Add the first squeeze coconut milk, more salt, if necessary, and allow to simmer till gravy reaches consistency required.

Steamed Ikan Bilis Sambal

1 lb (450 g) steamed ikan bilis,
    remove heads and
    intestines, wash and drain
2 red chillies and turmeric,
    the size of an almond,
    ground to a paste
Oil for frying
10 small onions, sliced finely
1 teaspoon dark soy sauce
    mixed with 2 dessertspoons
    water
Lime juice, to taste
Salt, if desired

Mix the fish with the ground chillies and turmeric. Heat about 3 dessertspoons oil in pan and then fry the fish till slightly crisp. Remove to platter.

Put a little more oil if necessary, fry the onions till soft. Put back the fish, add soy sauce and lime juice. Fry till a little dry, adding salt, if necessary.

Note:
Steamed ikan bilis is usually very salty. Add 2 fresh chillies, finely sliced, if you want a hotter sambal.

Indonesian Prawn Sambal

2 tablespoons vegetable oil
1 cup small onions, sliced
  finely
24 large fresh chillies, seeded,
  sliced finely and scalded in
  boiling water to remove the
  sting
1 kati (21 oz, 600 g) medium-
  sized fresh prawns, shelled
  and cleaned
1 piece of langkwas (galangal),
  bruised
½ teaspoon blachan mixed
  into a paste with water
2 - 3 teacups coconut milk
  (½ cup first squeeze, rest
  second) from 1 coconut
Salt to taste

Put oil in a pan. Fry onions and chillies till soft. Add prawns, langkuas, blachan and 2 cups second squeeze coconut milk. Allow to cook on very slow fire to make gravy red and to allow oil to rise to surface.

Add first squeeze coconut milk and remove gravy from fire after it boils.

Indonesian Coconut Sambal

2 dessertspoons oil
10 small onions, sliced finely
1 stalk serai (lemongrass),
  sliced very finely
2 tablespoons dried prawns,
  pounded
½ coconut (not too old),
  grated after dark skin has
  been removed
2 fresh red chillies, seeded
  and sliced finely
Salt

Put oil in pan, fry onions, sliced serai, and dried prawns. Add grated coconut and sliced chillies. Fry on very slow fire, stirring all the time till golden brown. Add salt to taste.

Note:
Make this the day before using and put in air-tight bottle.

Stuffed Sotong Sambal

12 large prawns, shelled,
  cleaned
Salt
Pepper
1 teaspoon chopped
  local celery
8 medium-sized sotong
  (squid), bodies about
  2½ - 3 in (6½ -7½ cm) long
3 dessertspoons oil

Finely ground together:
4 buah keras (candlenuts)
1 stalk serai (lemongrass),
  sliced
4 thick slices langkuas
  (galangal)
8 fresh red chillies, seeded
½ teaspoon blachan
10 small red onions

1½ teacups coconut from
  ½ coconut
Salt to taste

Chop prawns into small pieces and season with salt, pepper and chopped celery.

Remove head of sotong from body, cut away the bag of ink. Keep the body whole and clean out the inside. Thoroughly wash body and head in salt and then drain.

Stuff body of sotong with chopped prawns. Replace head and secure with toothpick. Fry stuffed sotong a little in hot oil (not deep). Put aside for use later.

Fry pounded ingredients in oil till well cooked. Add coconut milk and salt to taste. When sambal gravy is boiling put the stuffed sotong in and allow to simmer till nearly dry, turning sotong when necessary.

Note:
If desired, a little tamarind juice can be added to the gravy.

Sambal Blachan Omelette

3 dessertspoons oil
1 large onion, coarsely sliced
2 red fresh chillies and
  1 teaspoon roasted blachan,
  pounded to a paste
2 eggs, slightly beaten
Salt to taste

Heat oil in pan. Fry onions till soft, add the sambal blachan paste and when fragrant add beaten egg to which a little salt has been added. Turn omelette in portions as it cooks.

Serve hot with rice or bread.

Note:
For a mild flavour, seed chillies.

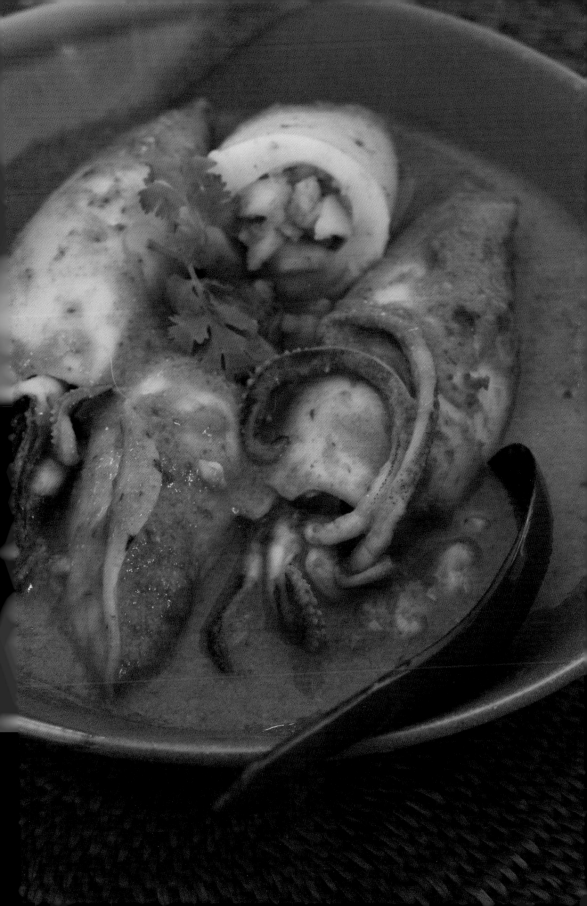

Indonesian Meat & Potato Cakes

Oil for frying
1½ dessertspoons chopped
    onions
¼ kati (5¼ oz, 150 g) beef or
    pork, minced
Salt and pepper to taste
2 medium-sized potatoes,
    boiled and mashed
1 teaspoon chopped local
    celery, if desired
2 eggs, beaten

Put a little butter or oil in frying pan, fry chopped onions, then the minced meat. Add salt and pepper. When cooked, remove meat on to plate and mix well with mashed potato and celery.

Add beaten egg and form into small cakes. Roll each in egg white and fry till well browned.

Tauhu Goreng

Hawker Style

8 squares taukwa (hard soya
    bean cake), fried crisp and
    sliced
½ kati (10½ oz, 300 g) taugeh
    (beansprouts), cleaned and
    scalded
2 cucumbers with skin on,
    washed and shredded

FOR SAUCE:
1 in (2½ cm) cube of
    gula melaka, crushed
1 teacup roasted peanuts,
    pounded finely
2 dessertspoons thick soya
    bean sauce
2 dessertspoons vinegar
¾ cup cold boiled water

Pounded together:
4 fresh green chillies
2 red chillies
1 clove garlic, if desired

Mix all the ingredients for sauce to a smooth consistency, adding more salt etc, to suit taste.

To serve, arrange a few pieces of fried taukwa in plate, sprinkle on top a little taugeh and shredded cucumber and pour over it some sauce.

Malay Kurmah

4 tablespoons ghee or butter,
   or 2 tablespoons butter and
   2 tablespoons vegetable oil
2 tablespoons finely sliced
   small onions

½ tablespoon finely sliced
   fresh ginger
2 in (5 cm) piece cinnamon
4 cloves
2 cardamoms
1 stem serai (lemongrass),
   bruised

Ground to a paste:
2 tablespoons ketumbar
   (coriander)
1 tablespoon jintan manis
   (anise)
1 tablespoon jintan puteh
   (cumin)
1 dessertspoon white
   peppercorns
6 buah keras (candlenuts)

½ kati (10½ oz, 300g) beef,
   mutton, lamb or chicken,
   cut into pieces
Salt to taste
2 - 3 cups coconut milk from
   ¾ coconut
Lime juice to taste

Put oil in pan. When hot fry sliced onions till slightly brown.

Add ginger, cinnamon, cloves, cardamons and serai.

Add ground ingredients, fry a little and then add meat and salt. Mix thoroughly and cover pan. Leave to cook for about 15 minutes.

Add coconut milk and allow to simmer slowly till gravy reaches consistency required.

Add lime juice to taste just before removing from fire.

Rendang

3 lb (1½ kg) beef, mutton,
   lamb or chicken, cut into
   small pieces
½ in (1¼ cm) langkwas
   (galangal), bruised
2 stalks serai (lemongrass),
   bruised

Ground together:
6 level tablespoons ketumbar
   (coriander)
1 tablespoon jintan manis
   (anise)
20 - 30 dried chillies, some
   seeded
1 teacup small red onions
2 - 3 cloves garlic, if desired
4 thin slices fresh ginger

4 teacups coconut milk from
   one grated coconut
Salt to taste
6 tablespoons grated
   coconut, roasted in dry
   pan over slow fire and then
   ground to a paste

Mix all the spices and ground ingredients with the meat in a pan.

Add the coconut milk and salt as required. Boil till meat is tender, reduce heat, add roasted grated coconut and cook till curry becomes dry, turning over the contents in the pan from time to time to prevent burning.

Curry Blandah

4 dessertspoons vegetable oil
2 cloves garlic, thinly sliced
4 dessertspoons sliced onions

Ground together:
4 dessertspoons ketumbar
  (coriander)
2 dessertspoons jintan puteh
  (cumin)
2 buah keras (candlenuts)
12 dried chillies
A piece of dry turmeric, the
  size of 2 peas

1 chicken (or 1 kati, 21 oz,
  600 g beef or pork), cut into
  pieces
Salt to taste
3 teacups coconut milk
  (1 cup first squeeze, rest
  second) from 1 coconut
1 stalk serai (lemongrass)
  bruised
1 slice (¼ in, 6 mm thick)
  langkwas (galangal)
Fried sliced onions for
  garnishing

Put oil in deep pan and when hot, fry the sliced garlic, when brown add sliced onions and when it it getting brown, add in ground ingredients, serai and langkwas.

Fry till oil begins to show and then add the meat. Stir well and after frying for about 10 minutes, add salt and 1 cup second squeeze coconut milk.

Cover pan and simmer till meat is tender. Then add the rest of the coconut milk and continue cooking.

When gravy has reached the consistency you require, serve with a sprinkling of fried onions.

Liver Curry

3 dessertspoons oil
10 small onions, sliced

Ground finely:
1 teaspoon ketumbar
   (coriander)
½ teaspoon jintan puteh
   (cumin)
½ teaspoon jintan manis
   (anise)
1 stalk serai (lemongrass)
4 chillies
1 clove garlic, if desired
1 in (2½ cm) cube burnt
   coconut

1 lb (450 g) liver, cut into
   small pieces
1½ teacups coconut milk
   from ½ coconut

Put oil in pan. When hot add sliced onions. Add and fry the ground ingredients till well done. Add liver, stirring well. Add a little coconut milk at first, then add the rest.

Allow to simmer till liver is cooked. (Amount of gravy depends on individual taste).

Satay

1½ lb (680 g) beef, lamb, pork or chicken, cut into small pieces

Finely ground together:
1 dessertspoon ketumbar (coriander), roasted in a dry pan
1 teaspoon jintan puteh (cumin), roasted in a dry pan
1 teaspoon jintan manis (anise), roasted in a dry pan
Turmeric, size of 2 peas
Kenchor (*Kaempferia galangal*), size of 2 peas, optional
2 dried red chillies
1 stalk serai (lemongrass)
2 thin slices langkwas (galangal)

1 teaspoon sugar
1 teaspoon thick tamarind juice
Salt to taste

Mixed together for basting:
¼ cup first squeeze coconut milk from ½ grated coconut
2 dessertspoons vegetable oil

Mix the meat, which has been cut into small pieces, the ground ingredients, sugar, tamarind juice and salt.

Put seasoned meat on fine metal skewers or coconut leaf stems. Allow meat to stand for an hour or so before grilling on coal fire.

When grilling the satay, baste meat with coconut milk and oil mixture.

Note:
Satay may be grilled over a gas cooker or electric cooker but you will not get the same flavour in the meat as you would from using a coal fire.

See page 176 for recipe for Satay Sauce.

Satay Sauce

1 dessertspoon vegetable oil

Ground to a smooth paste:
1 dessertspoon ketumbar
  (coriander)
1 teaspoon jintan puteh
  (cumin)
1 teaspoon jintan manis
  (anise)
10 red dried chillies, seeded
  if you want a mild flavour
1 clove garlic
12 small onions
1 teaspoon blachan
4 buah keras (candlenut)
1 stalk serai (lemongrass)

1 teacup roasted peanuts,
  pounded or ground
1¼ teacup coconut milk from
  ½ coconut
½ teacup tamarind juice
Salt to taste
1 teaspoon sugar, or to taste
8 blimbings, each cut into
  two, lengthwise or
4 medium sized tomatoes
  cut into wedges, or a little
  of each

Heat oil in pan. Fry ground ingredients till well cooked and fragrant. Add ground peanuts, stir, adding coconut milk gradually. Add tamarind juice, salt and sugar to taste. When boiling, add blimbing and/or tomatoes and allow to simmer till oil rises to the top.

Remove to deep dish and serve with grilled satay.

Slices of cucumber and 2 large onions cut into wedges can be serve with satay.

Note:
The roasted peanuts must be pounded or ground not too fine. It must be grainy, not a paste.

Vegetable Curry (1)

2 dessertspoons oil

Ground together:
3 buah keras (candlenuts)
4 - 6 fresh red chillies
1 teaspoon blachan
10 small onions

¼ kati (5¼ oz, 150 g) fresh
   prawns, shelled and
   cleaned
1½ coconut milk (½ cup first
   squeeze, rest second) from
   ½ coconut
1 small sweet potato, cut into
   small pieces
½ kati (10½ oz, 300 g) kangkong
   (water convolvulous), cut
   into pieces
Salt to taste

Put oil in deep pan and when hot fry the ground ingredients well.

Add prawns and when cooked add the thin coconut milk and the sweet potato and cook till half done. Add kangkong, cover pan and cook till vegetable is soft.

Add thick coconut milk, adding more salt if necessary, and simmer for a few minutes.

Note:
½ kati (10½ oz, 300 g) sayoh manis (*Sauropus androgynus*) or pak-choy can be used instead of kangkong. Serve these vegetable curries with Salted Fish Roe Sambal (page 139).

Vegetable Curry (2)

2 dessertspoons oil

Ground together:
4 chillies or 1½ teaspoons
   pepper
2 teaspoons blachan
10 small onions, not too fine

3 oz (85 g) dried prawns,
   cleaned
2 cups water
Salt to taste
1 lb (450 g) of any vegetable –
   brinjals, ladies fingers,
   sayoh manis, long beans,
   pumpkin or vegetable
   marrow, cut into pieces

Heat oil in pan. Fry ground ingredients. Then add dried prawns and after a few minutes add water and little salt. When boiling add vegetables.

Note:
Pumpkin and long beans make a good mixture. When using sayoh manis (*Sauropus androgynus*) add a few pieces sweet potato.

Vegetable & Prawn Curry

Ingredients A:
½ in (1¼ cm) fresh turmeric
4 buah keras (candlenuts)
4 slices langkwas (galangal)

Ingredients B:
10 fresh chillies or less,
  seeded
½ teaspoon blachan
15 small onions

4 dessertspoons cooking oil
½ kati (10½ oz, 300 g) prawns,
  shelled and cleaned
Salt to taste
2 teacups coconut milk
  (first and second squeeze)
  from ½ coconut
¾ kati (1 lb, 480 g) French
  beans, cleaned and cut into
  1 in (2½ cm) pieces

Pound A till fine. Add B and continue pounding.

Put oil in pan. Fry pounded ingredients till well done. Add prawns and salt, stirring well. Add second squeeze coconut milk and, when boiling, add French beans and cover pan till beans are a little soft.

Remove cover, add first squeeze coconut milk and leave to simmer for a few minutes.

Note:
Any vegetable can be used for this type of curry.

Vegetable Dish

2 dessertspoons oil

Ground finely together:
1 small piece of turmeric
4 fresh red chillies, seeded
2 slices ginger
12 small onions

¾ kati (1 lb, 480 g) French
  beans, cut into small pieces
1 tomato, sliced
Salt to taste
½ cup water

Put oil in pan and when hot, fry ground ingredients till well cooked. Add French beans, tomato and salt. Stir well.

Add water and cover pan. Leave to cook for about 10 minutes. Remove cover and cook till vegetable is tender and dry.

For variety:
Replace French beans with cauliflower and frozen peas.

Indonesain Style Long Beans in Gravy

2 dessertspoons oil

Pounded fine:
2 - 4 red fresh chillies, seeded
2 buah keras (candlenut)
½ teaspoon blachan
10 small onions

150 g small fresh prawns,
    shelled and cleaned
1 cup first squeeze, 1 cup
    second squeeze coconut
    milk from ½ coconut
150 g long beans, cut into
    2 cm lengths
2 hard soya bean cakes, cut
    into small cubes
Salt

Put oil in deep pan. Fry pounded ingredients till well cooked. Add prawns and after about five minutes, add second squeeze coconut milk. Add beans and soya bean cake and salt.

When beans are tender add the first squeeze coconut milk and simmer till it boils.

Zuberbuhler Special

An imitation of Sukiyaki

1 chicken, 1½ kati (2 lb, 900 g)
Salt and pepper to taste
1 stalk spring onions
1 stalk local celery
4 dessertspoons butter
4 large onions, slice these in
   rather thick slices
¼ - ½ cup soya sauce (not the
   very thick kind)

About a cup of each of
the following vegetables:
Cabbage, sliced in thick slices
Spring onions, cut in 1½ in
   (3 cm) lengths
French beans, cut in 1½ in
   (3 cm) lengths
Cauliflower in small pieces
Button mushrooms
Sliced tomatoes
Green peas

6 eggs

Remove meat from bones. Cut meat into small pieces and put aside. Boil bones in 6 - 8 teacups water, seasoned with salt, pepper, spring onions and local celery.

Put butter in pan which is not too deep and which has a large mouth. Fry sliced onions till they are soft.

Add chicken, fry for about 10 minutes. Then add soya sauce and mix well. Add chicken stock and, when boiling, add vegetables, keeping chicken and each vegetable in its own place. Add more salt, if necessary. Do not stir. When vegetables are cooked, add eggs, one at a time, whole, in a depression, made here and there. When eggs are cooked according to the fancy of each person, the dish is ready for eating.

Serve with plain boiled rice and any of the following sauces:-
Mustard seasoned with vinegar and salt
Chilli sauce
Tomato sauce
Sweet and sour sauce

For variety:
Add 1 dessertspoon sugar if you like the dish sweet. Substitute thin slices of beef for chicken.

Note:
This is a dish for a cold evening as it is cooked at the table on a small electric plate around which the family sit and help themselves from the pan itself.

Siamese Curry

1 coconut for milk,
  1 teacup first squeeze,
  2 cups second squeeze
1½ teaspoons salt
1 lb (450 g) beef rump, cut
  into small, thin pieces
  (1 x 1 x ¼ in, 2½ x 2½ x ½ cm)

Finely ground together:
3 level dessertspoons
  ketumbar (coriander)
1 teaspoon jintan puteh
  (cumin)
1 teaspoon jintan manis
  (anise)
1 teaspoon peppercorns
8 dried red chillies
4 cardamoms
4 cloves
Nutmeg, size of green pea
Star anise, 2 points
1 stalk serai (lemongrass)
4 thin slices langkwas
  (galangal)
1 teaspoon blachan

3 green brinjals, cut into two
  lengthwise and then into
  pieces across 1cm thick.
  Soak in water before using.
3 limau perot (kaffir lime)
  leaves, broken into small
  pieces
Selaseh (basil) leaves from
  4 stalks
4 green chillies cut into two
  lengthwise and seeded,
  unless you want hot curry

Put the cup of thick coconut milk in pan and bring to the boil. Add 1½ teaspoons salt and add meat. Allow to cook on slow fire till the coconut milk becomes oil.

Add the ground ingredients and stir well, frying till well done and fragrant.

Add the remaining 2 cups of coconut milk and, when boiling, add the brinjal, flavouring leaves and green chillies.

Simmer till brinjal is cooked, adding more salt if necessary.

Devil

2 dessertspoons vegetable oil
1 large onion, sliced in rather
  thick slices
2 slices ginger, coarsely
  shredded
1 tomato, cut into wedges

Ground together:
2 dried chillies
Dry turmeric, the size of a pea
6 small red onions
1 clove garlic
½ teaspoon blachan, optional
2 buah keras (candlenuts),
  optional

½ lb (225 g) cold roast
  chicken, mutton, beef or
  pork, cut into thin slices
1 teaspoon mustard
2 dessertspoons vinegar
1 teaspoon sugar, more if
  desired
Salt to taste

Put oil in pan. When hot, add sliced ingredients, and after frying for about five minutes, add ground ingredients. Fry a little longer, add meat and cook for about 10 minutes.

Add mustard, vinegar, sugar and salt to taste. Add 2 dessertspoons or so of gravy from meat, if available.

Note:
This is an Eurasian curry dish

Indian Dishes

Mango Chutney

6 green mangoes
2 cloves garlic
¼ oz (7 g) fresh ginger
2 oz (55 g) preserved ginger
12 almonds
10 dried chillies, seeded
½ cup white vinegar
1¼ cups sugar
1½ dessertspoons salt,
  or to taste
2 dessertspoons raisins

Peel and slice mangoes. Slice the garlic, the fresh and preserved ginger. Blanch and slice the almonds, lengthwise. Grind chillies to a smooth paste.

Boil vinegar, sugar and salt till it begins to thicken. Add ground chillies, garlic and ginger stirring well and, after 10 minutes, add mango slices. Boil till they begin to be transparent.

Add raisins and almonds and, when boiling, remove from fire and pour into bottles. Cover bottles.

Note:
Do not overboil if you wish to keep mango in slices.

Pineapple & Apple Chutney

½ cup white vinegar
1½ cups sugar
1¼ dessertspoons salt,
  or to taste
½ teaspoon ground cinnamon

Finely ground:
12 dried chillies, seeded
½ oz (15 g) fresh ginger
2 cloves garlic

2 cups fresh pineapple,
  finely diced
2 apples, removed skin and
  core and cut into pieces
½ cup raisins, whole
2 dessertspoons preserved
  ginger, shredded

Put in deep enamel pan the vinegar, sugar, salt, cinnamon and ground spices and bring to the boil.

Add the pineapple, apple, raisins and ginger. Boil slowly, stirring often to prevent burning, till apple is broken up and the chutney reaches a thick consistency. (The pineapple will remain in pieces). Put into bottles and cover. This chutney will keep for months.

Serve with rice and curry or with meat loaf, roast chicken, etc. It adds taste to dull dishes.

Note:
You can substitute 2 teaspoons powdered chilli, ½ teaspoon powdered ginger and ¼ teaspoon powdered garlic for the fresh.

Pickles

This is a basic recipe for pickles. You may use it for young green mangoes, limes, rembunia, blimbing, brinjal and even salted fish or salted fish roe. These ingredients must be preserved befor pickling.

To preserve mango:
Use 12 green mangoes to make 2 teacups dry mango preserve. Halve, remove seeds and cut each half into 4 pieces lengthwise. Place in porcelain basin, sprinkle on top 2 tablespoons salt. Shake the bowl so that mango gets thoroughly mixed with salt. Place porcelain bowl in hot sun every day, until mango is dry enough for use, shake the bowl to mix contents once in a while.

To preserve rembunia (kundang, Bouea macrophylla):
Use 1½ kati (2 lb, 900 g) small green rembunia.
Halve each fruit and remove seeds. Use same method of preserving as for mango (see above).

To preserve blimbing:
Add salt to blimbing. This has more water than mango or rembunia. When drying in the sun spread blimbing on flat basket. Leave porcelain bowl in the sun too, so that the liquid can evaporate. Put blimbing in liquid during the night.

To preserve limes:
Cut each lime ¾ way up from the bottom into four sections. Use the same method as for mango.

To preserve brinjals:
Brinjal makes a good pickle but it will not keep as long as mango or lime pickle. 5 young green brinjals will be enough for ingredients given in recipe. Cut brinjal into pieces 1½ x ½ in (3 x 1 cm) after removing all seeds in the centre. Dry pieces of brinjal in hot sun for two hours before using.

To preserve salted fish or salted fish roe:
Wash salted fish and dry in the sun. Cut into small pieces and fry a little before putting into pickle gravy.

FOR PICKLING:
¾ **cup good vegetable oil**
4 slices fresh ginger, ground
to measure 1 teaspoon
12 slices ginger, coarsely
shredded
12 - 16 cloves garlic, coarsely
shredded
1 teapoon alba (brown mustard
seeds), whole
1 dessertspoon mustard
seed, ground separately
and not too finely

Ground together, using
vinegar for softening spices
during grinding:
20 dried chillies, half of them
seeded
2½ tablespoons jintan puteh
(cumin)
1 in (2½ cm) piece turmeric

1½ teacups vinegar, more if
necessary
2 tablespoons sugar, or to
taste
Salt to taste

2 teacups of any one of the
preserved ingredients

Put oil in pan. Fry ground ginger and shredded ginger and garlic. Remove ginger and garlic from oil after about 2 minutes. Set aside for later use.

Fry alba, ground mustard seeds and all other ground spices in the same oil, stirring well, till well cooked. Add vinegar, sugar, and a little salt. Allow to simmer for a few minutes.

Add the fried ginger and garlic and the preserved ingredient which has been scalded with boiling water and drained. Stir, adding more sugar and salt if necessary.

When boiling, transfer pickles to porcelain bowl and allow to cool before putting away in bottle.

Mild Curry Powder

For any kind of meat

1 kati (21 oz, 600 g) ketumbar
  (coriander)
¾ kati (1 lb, 450 g) jintan
  puteh (cumin)
½ kati (10½ oz, 300 g) jintan
  manis (anise)
¼ kati (5¼ oz, 150 g) dried
  chillies, seeded
¼ kati (5¼ oz, 150 g) dry
  turmeric
1½ in (3 cm) cinnamon
8 cloves
2 dessertspoons peppercorns

Wash each ingredients well, removing all grit.

Dry thoroughly in the sun, using large flat cane-fibre trays, for two or three days.

Roast in dry pan over slow fire in small quantities, till spices begin to smell good, stirring all the times. See that spices do not burn. Then take the roasted spices to the mill to be ground into fine powder. Pick into air-tight bottles for future use.

Notes:

If curry powder is made well it will keep for a long time.

If you like the flavour of cardamoms and nutmeg add these spices whole to curry during cooking.

Hot Curry Powder

For any kind of meat

1 kati (21 oz, 600 g) ketumbar
  (coriander)
¾ kati (1 lb, 450 g) jintan
  puteh (cumin)
½ kati (10½ oz, 300 g) jintan
  manis (anise)
¾ kati (1 lb, 450 g) dried
  chillies, seeded
¼ kati (5¼ oz, 150 g) dry
  turmeric
1½ in (3 cm) cinnamon
8 cloves
2 dessertspoons peppercorns

Wash each ingredients well, removing all grit.

Dry thoroughly in the sun, using large flat cane-fibre trays, for two or three days.

Roast in dry pan over slow fire in small quantities, till spices begin to smell good, stirring all the times. See that spices do not burn. Then take the roasted spices to the mill to be ground into fine powder. Pick into air-tight bottles for future use.

Note:

If you like the flavour of cardamoms and nutmeg add these spices whole to curry during cooking.

Curry Powder for Fish or Prawn Curry

1¼ kati (26 oz, 750 g) ketumbar
(coriander)
¾ kati (1 lb, 450 g) jintan
puteh (cumin)
¼ kati (5¼ oz, 150 g) dried
chillies, seeded
¼ kati (5¼ oz, 150 g) dry
turmeric
2 dessertspoons peppercorns

Wash each ingredients well, removing all grit.

Dry thoroughly in the sun, using large flat cane-fibre trays, for two or three days.

Roast in dry pan over slow fire in small quantities, till spices begin to smell good, stirring all the times. See that spices do not burn. Then take the roasted spices to the mill to be ground into fine powder. Pick into air-tight bottles for future use.

Note:
If you like the flavour of cardamoms and nutmeg add these spices whole to curry during cooking.

Chilli Sauce (1)

2½ cups vinegar, ¼ cup of
which can be used for
grinding chillies etc.
2 cups sugar
1½ dessertspoons salt

*Ingredients to be finely
ground, each separately:*
60 large dried chillies, seeded
to make 1 cup
8 small cloves garlic
2 in (5 cm) fresh ginger
1 cup raisins
1 cup sultanas

Mix all ingredients in enamel pan and bring to boil. Allow to simmer for about ½ hour, stirring to prevent boiling over, and adding more salt and sugar, if necessary.

Note:
This is a thick chilli sauce and should be kept in a bottle with large neck.

Chilli Sauce (2)

Ground finely together:
60 (9 oz, 250 g) large dried
   chillies, seeded
8 cloves garlic
2 in (5 cm) fresh ginger

2 cups vinegar
2½ cups sugar, or to taste
1½ dessertspoons salt

Mix all ingredients and boil on slow fire until it thickens, adding more salt and sugar, if necessary.

Note:
Seeded fresh red chillies can be used instead of the dried.

Spicy Potato Dish

Spice mix:
1 dessertspoon ketumbar
   (coriander)
1 teaspoon jintan puteh
   (cumin)
1 teaspoon jintan manis
   (anise)
1 teaspoon kas-kas
   (poppy seeds)

1 lb (450 g) medium-sized
   potatoes, skinned and each
   cut into 8 pieces
1 teaspoon powdered
   turmeric
Salt
1 teaspoon jintan puteh
   (cumin), whole
1 cup oil
2 dessertspoons diced onions
1 teaspoon shredded fresh
   ginger
4 red chillies, ground to a
   smooth paste
½ cup water

Roast the spice mix a few seconds in dry pan till fragrant and then coarsely pounded in dry pestle and mortar. Set aside.

Put cut potatoes in a dish, add the powered turmeric, a dessertspoon salt and the jintan puteh. After 15 minutes, drain potatoes in colander.

Heat the oil in frying pan. Fry the potatoes a little at a time, till cooked and golden brown, and remove from oil to a plate.

Put about 2 tablespoons of the oil that has been used for frying potatoes in a pan, fry the onions till they are soft, add the shredded ginger and pounded chillies and, after a few seconds, ½ cup of water.

When boiling put in the fried potatoes and cook on slow fire, stirring now and then till dry, adding more salt, if necessary. Stir in the pounded dry spice mix just before serving.

Vegetable Sothi

2½ cups coconuts milk (1 cup first squeeze, rest second squeeze) from 1 coconut
½ teaspoon alba (brown mustard seeds), optional
1½ teaspoons turmeric powder
2 sprigs curry leaves
Salt
1 lb (450 g) medium-sized fresh prawns, shelled and cleaned
¼ lb (115 g) potatoes, cut into pieces
¼ lb (115 g) cabbage, cut into pieces
¼ lb (115 g) French beans, sliced
¼ lb (115 g) small ladies fingers, whole
3 red and 3 green fresh chillies, coarsely sliced
2 large onions, cut into wedges
2 dessertspoons lime juice, or to taste

Put in deep pan the second squeeze coconut milk, alba, turmeric, curry leaves and onions and bring to the boil. Add 1½ dessertspoons salt and the prawns. After a few seconds add potatoes and, when these are half cooked, add all the other vegetables, chillies and onions. Simmer till vegetables are done.

Add in first squeeze of coconut milk, stirring gently to prevent curdling. When gravy boils, remove pan from fire and add lime juice and more salt, if necessary.

For variety:
You may leave out prawns if you want a purely vegetable dish.

Use ikan kurau (threadfin) if you prefer fish to prawns, but add the coarsely diced ikan kurau after vegetables are cooked and before adding the first squeeze of coconut milk.

Spinach in Coconut Milk

1¼ lb (570 g) young spinach,
  cleaned and shredded
Salt to taste
3 dessertspoons vegetable oil
10 small onions, finely sliced
6 dried red chillies, each
  broken into two
1 level teaspoon mustard
  seed
½ lb (225 g) fresh prawns,
  shelled, cleaned and diced
½ teaspoon turmeric powder
1½ teacups coconut milk,
  from ¾ coconut
Browned sliced onions for
  garnishing

Put shredded spinach in boiling water with a little salt, cover pan and cook for about 10 minutes. Pour into colander to drain away all water, pressing spinach down with wooden spoon.

Heat oil in pan, fry onions till soft and add dried chillies, mustard seeds, prawns. Add spinach, salt and turmeric powder. Stir well and add coconut milk and allow to simmer for about 10 minutes.

Put into dish and decorate top with browned onions.

For variety:
Add curry leaves if you like the flavour.

Vegetable Dish

2 tablespoons vegetable oil
10 small onions, coarsely
  sliced
2 fresh red chillies, coarsely
  sliced
1 teaspoon mustard seeds
½ lb (225 g) prawns, shelled,
  cleaned and diced
1 lb (450 g) French beans, cut
  into 3cm lengths and
  coarsely shredded and diced
½ - ¾ teaspoon turmeric
  powder
Salt to taste
1½ cups coconut milk (½ cup
  first squeeze, rest recond
  squeeze) from ¾ coconut
Lime juice to taste
Sugar to taste

Heat the oil in the pan. Fry onions till soft, add chillies, curry leaves and mustard seeds. Fry a little, then add prawns and, when cooked, add the French beans, powdered turmeric, salt and the second squeeze of coconut milk. Cover pan and allow vegetable to cook for about ten minutes.

Remove cover, add thick coconut milk and stir gently till it begins to boil. Remove pan from fire and add lime juice.

For variety:
You can use shredded cabbage or string beans instead of French beans.

If you use ladies fingers, cut into 1½ in (4 cm) lengths after washing and roast in dry pan, stirring once in a while. This will congeal the slimy fluid in the vegetable. Do not worry if the vegetables burns a little.

Brinjal Sandwiches

2 large brinjals, green or
  purple
1 teacup besan (gram flour)
1 cup water
1 teaspoon baking powder
Salt to taste
2 large onions, cut into two
  from top to bottom, and
  then finely sliced
2 or more red and green fresh
  chillies, finely sliced
Vegetable oil for deep frying

Cut brinjals into thin slices, every two pieces to be joined together at one end to hold them together. Put into cold water to soak.

Mix besan with 1 cup water to make a smooth paste. Add baking powder and salt to taste. Set aside.

Remove brinjal from water. Wash and drain and rub a little salt on and between slices. Place in each sandwich a few slices of onions and chillies, hold pieces firmly together, dip in besan batter and fry in deep hot oil. Turn over when necessary. When brown, remove, drain on paper and serve.

Putchree

4 tablespoon oil
10 small onions, finely sliced
6 cloves garlic, coarsely sliced
1 cm piece fresh ginger,
  coarsely sliced

Curry paste to be made of:
1 dessertspoons ketumbar
1 dessertspoon jintan puteh
½ dessertspoon jintan manis
8 dried chillies
Piece of turmeric,
  size of 2 peas

2 cups thick tamarind juice
from 1½ dessertspoons
  tamarind
2 tablespoons sugar, or to
  taste
Salt to taste
4 green brinjals
3 green and 3 red chillies, slit
  half way up
2 sprigs curry leaves, optional

Cut brinjal into halves and then each piece into two. Make two cuts, half way up each piece and then soak in water for half an hour. Wash before using

Heat oil in pan, fry sliced onions till soft. Add garlic and ginger and curry paste. Fry till fragrant and then add tamarind juice, salt and sugar to taste. Add brinjal and chillies, simmer till cooked but firm. Do not overcook.

Serve with any kind of rich rice dish like briani, pilau and yellow rice.

Note:
This is a pickled vegetable dish and keeps for 2 or 3 days.

For variety:
You can use pineapple instead of brinjal. This keeps longer than brinjal.

Dhall & Meat Cakes

½ lb (225 g) beef or mutton, diced
¼ lb (115 g) dhall (lentils), washed and drained
Salt to taste
2 dessertspoons oil
1 tablespoons diced onions
2½ dessertspoons curry powder made into paste with a little water
2 tablespoons water
2 eggs

Onions, thicky sliced
Red and green chillies, thickly sliced
Lime, sliced

Boil meat and lentils till well cooked, adding a little salt. Remove from fire and when cool, pass through a fine mincer or grind on a grinding stone till fine and soft.

Put 2 dessertspoons oil in pan, fry diced onions till slightly brown, and then add curry paste and about 2 tablespoons water. Mix this with the ground meat and lentils, adding the beaten eggs and salt. Shape into cakes about half an inch thick, roll in beaten egg white and fry in oil till brown. Drain on paper.

Serve with thinly sliced onions, thinly sliced fresh red and green chillies, slices of lime.

Watery Dhall
To be served with a dry curry

1 tablespoon oil or ghee
2 cloves garlic, finely minced
1 large onion, diced
1 piece turmeric, size of an almond, finely ground
10 dried red chillies, seeded and finely ground with 1 dessertspoon jintan puteh (cumin)
2 medium-sized tomatoes, diced
1 cup dhall (red or yellow lentils), cleaned, washed and drained
Salt to taste
2 cups water

Put oil in deep pan. When hot, brown garlic and onions. Add turmeric and chilli paste and a tablespoon of water. Then add tomato, dhall and salt.

Fry for 5 minutes and then add the water and allow to simmer till required consistency is reached.

Dhall-Cha

3 dessertspoons oil
10 small onions, finely sliced
2 cloves garlic, finely sliced

Freshly ground curry paste of:
1 dessertspoon ketumbar
  (coriander)
1 dessertspoons jintan puteh
  (cumin)
½ dessertspoon jintan manis
  (anise)
Turmeric, size of 2 peas
10 dried chillies
2 slices ginger

½ cup dhall of any kind,
  soaked in cold water
2 potatoes, cut into small
  pieces
2 - 2½ cups thin tamarind
  juice, from 1 dessertspoon
  tamarind
Salt to taste
3 green brinjals cut into
  small pieces, soaked in
  water before use
2 tomatoes cut into small
  pieces
2 red and 2 green fresh
  chillies, slit halfway down
  middle

Heat oil. Fry onions and garlic till brown. Add curry paste and after 5 minutes, add the dhall and one cup water. When dhall is soft, add potatoes and, when almost cooked, add the tamarind juice and salt.

When boiling, add brinjals, tomatoes and chillies and simmer till they are cooked but firm.

Dry Dhall

1 cup dhall (red or yellow
  lentils)
2 tablespoons oil or ghee
1 dessertspoon diced onions
2 cloves garlic, finely minced
4 red dried chillies ground
  together with 1 dessertspoon jintan puteh (cumin)
1 piece turmeric, size of an
  almond, ground to a
  smooth paste
1 large red tomato, diced
Salt to taste
Water, sufficient to cover
  dhall

Thoroughly clean dhall, wash, soak in cold water for
1½ hours and drain.

Heat oil in deep pan. Fry diced onions and garlic till
golden brown. Add chilli and turmeric paste and after
frying for a few second, add tomato and dhall.

Fry a little, add salt and just enough water to cover
dhall. Cook over quick fire till dhall is soft. Then
reduce heat and allow dhall to cook very slowly till
it is dry.

This is a dry dhall. Remove pan from fire when dhall
is just cooked, but dry and grainy. Do not stir too
much as you want the dhall to be grainy.

Note:
You can substitute 2 teaspoons chilli powder, 1
teaspoon cumin powder and 1 teaspoon turmeric
powder mixed into a paste with some water for the
freshly ground chillies and turmeric.

Indian Kurmah

3 dessertspoons ghee, or
  more if you like
2 cloves garlic, sliced
16 small onions, sliced
½ in (1¼ cm) ginger, sliced
1 in (2½ cm) piece of cinnamon
3 cloves
3 cardamoms

Ground together:
2 tablespoons ketumbar
  (coriander)
1 tablespoon jintan puteh
  (cumin)
1 dessertspoon jintan manis
  (anise)
1 dessertspoon white
  peppercorns
¾ in (2 cm) piece turmeric

2 katis (2½ lb, 1.2 kg) of
  mutton, beef or chicken,
  cut into pieces
Salt to taste
2 - 3 teacups milk to which
  juice of lime has been
  added to curdle it
20 blanched almonds, ground
  separately
2 bundles of small coriander
  leaves

Put ghee in deep pan and, when hot, fry the sliced garlic, onion and ginger till slightly brown. Add the cinnamon, cloves and cardamoms, and then the ground spices.

When cooked add the meat and salt: stir well, and allow to cook for about 15 minutes in covered pan.

Add a little water and cook. When meat is tender add the milk to which the ground almonds (and kas-kas if mutton is used) have been mixed. When gravy has reached the consistency desired, add the coriander leaves and stir well.

Note:
If you are making mutton kurmah, add 1 dessertspoon kas-kas (poppy seeds), ground separately.

Dry Curry
North Indian Style

4 dessertspoons ghee or oil
2 large onions, diced
16 - 20 dried chillies, seeded
  and ground
½ teaspoon ground fresh
  ginger
1½ in (4 cm) cinnamon
4 cloves
1 chicken or 2 lb (900 g) beef,
  mutton or pork
¾ in (340 g) red tomatoes, cut
  into pieces
Salt to taste

Put ghee in pan. Fry diced onions till a little brown. Add ground chillies and ginger, cinnamon and cloves. Add meat, stir well, then put in tomatoes. Add salt to taste. Allow to cook till curry is dry.

For variety:
Chicken livers done this way are good. Cut each into two.

Minced Meat Curry

2 dessertspoons oil
3 tablespoons finely sliced
  small onions
½ tablespoon shredded ginger
A small piece of cinnamon
4 cloves
4 cardamoms

*Ground together
  after dry frying:*
2 dessertspoons ketumbar
  (coriander)
1 dessertspoon jintan puteh
  (cumin)
1 teaspoon jintan manis (anise)
8 - 10 dried chillies
A piece of turmeric, size of
  2 peas

1 lb (450 g) minced beef, lamb
  or pork
Salt to taste
1 teacup milk from ¼ coconut
  or 2 tomatoes, sliced

Heat oil in pan, brown onions, add ginger and whole spices. Add curry paste and when fragrant add minced meat and salt. Stir, cover pan and after 15 minutes, add either coconut milk or tomatoes. Continue cooking till quite dry. Serve with rice and Watery Dhall (page 198).

Note:
Curried mince may be used as filling for curry puffs, Choux Pastry or sandwiches.

Beef Curry

3 tablespoons vegetable oil
2 cloves garlic, sliced
4 dessertspoons sliced
  onions
2 slices fresh ginger, shredded
6 dessertspoons curry
  powder made into paste
  with water
1 small piece cinnamon
2 cloves
2 lb (900 g) beef, cut into
  pieces
Salt to taste
3 - 4 teacups coconut milk
  from 1 coconut
½ - 1 lb (225 - 450 g) potatoes,
  cut into pieces
2 - 3 tomatoes, if desired

Put oil in pan when hot, fry sliced garlic till brown; then add sliced onions, and, when slightly brown, add ginger.

Add curry paste and cinnamon and cloves. Fry a little.

Add beef and salt. Stir and leave to simmer for about 10 minutes.

Add a cupful or so of coconut milk. Cover and allow to simmer till meat is tender.

Add another cupful or so of coconut milk, potatoes and tomatoes. Cover and leave to cook on slow fire till potatoes are cooked and gravy reaches consistency required.

For variety:
If you like tomatoes, leave out coconut milk altogether, and use 1 lb (450 g) tomatoes.

Chicken, mutton or pork can be be used instead of beef.

Notes:
Milk (diluted evaporated or fresh) can be used as substitute for coconut milk. If a very thick gravy is required, use more curry powder and less coconut milk.

If you want freshly ground curry paste grind:
4 dessertspoons ketumbar (coriander)
2 dessertspoons jintan puteh (cumin)
1 dessertspoon jintan manis (anise)
16 dried red chillies, seeded
1 teaspoon peppercorns
A pice of turmeric, size of almond
Small piece cinnamon
4 cloves
4 cardamoms

Beef Ball Curry

(A) Mix together:

1 lb (450 g) minced beef
1 dessertspoon very finely
  chopped onions
2 thin slices ginger, very
  finely chopped
1 teaspoon salt
1 dessertspoon dry curry
  powder

4 tablespoons cooking oil
3 cloves garlic, sliced
4 dessertspoons sliced onions
2 slices ginger, shredded
4 dessertspoons curry
  powder made into paste
  with water
2 teacups coconut milk
  (½ cup first squeeze, 1½
  cups second squeeze) from
  ½ coconut
2 or 3 tomatoes, if required,
  cut into small pieces
Curry leaves, if you like the
  flavour

Mix (A) well with fingers, roll into compact balls, and place on a plate.

Put oil in pan and when hot, fry garlic till brown, add sliced onions and then ginger. When slightly brown, add curry paste, and stir well, adding a little thin coconut milk.

Add the rest of the thin coconut milk and salt to taste. When boiling, add meat balls, one by one, and the tomatoes.

When meat balls are firm, add curry leaves, thick coconut milk and leave curry to boil till desired consistency is reached.

Vindaloo (1)

3 - 4 dessertspoons
   vegetable oil
4 cloves garlic, ground
   separately
12 small red onions, sliced

(A) Ground together:
3 dessertspoons jintan puteh
   (cumin)
20 dried chillies, seeded
1 small piece of turmeric

1½ teaspoons fresh ginger,
   ground separately
1 teaspoon mustard seeds,
   ground coarsely, separately
1 chicken (about 1½ lb, 680 g),
   cut into pieces
Salt to taste
4 - 5 dessertspoons vinegar
Sugar to taste

Put oil in pan. Fry ground garlic till slightly brown. Fry sliced onions then add ground ingredients (A). Add ground ginger and mustard seeds.

Add chicken and salt. Fry a few minutes, add a little water, and cover pan.

When chicken is almost cooked, add vinegar and sugar, according to taste.

Simmer till chicken is tender.

Notes:
Vindaloo, or pickled meat, is a dry curry.

Do not do not seed chillies if a hotter curry is desired.

Vindaloo (2)

1 chicken (about 1½ lb, 680 g),
   cut into pieces or equal
   weight of pork or beef
1 dessertspoon mustard
   seeds, crushed
1 teaspoon white vinegar
¾ teacup vegetable oil
¾ teacup sugar, or to taste
Salt to taste

Ground together finely:
16 dried chillies, with or
   without seeds, to taste
1 dessertspoon jintan puteh
   (cumin)
Turmeric, size of an almond
6 cloves garlic

Mix all ingredients and leave in porcelain dish for 2 hours. Then bring to boil, reduce heat and simmer gently till tender, adding sugar and salt, if necessary.

Notes:
The pieces of meat should be wiped dry before mixing with ingredients.

Use part of vinegar to grind spices. Do not use water if you want to keep vindaloo for a few days.

Fish Chilli Curry

4 teacups coconut milk
(1 cup first squeeze, rest
second squeeze) from one
coconut
20 dried chillies, seeded,
ground finely
¾ teacup small onions, sliced
finely
½ in (1¼ cm) piece of fresh
ginger, shredded
3 or 4 sprigs curry leaves
Salt to taste
1 kati (21 oz, 600 g) ikan kurau
(threadfin), cut into pieces

Mix together in pan 3 teacups second squeeze coconut milk with the ground chillies, sliced onions, ginger, curry leaves and salt. Cook over slow fire and when it boils add fish.

When fish is cooked add the thick coconut milk, stirring gently to prevent milk curdling. When gravy boils remove pan from fire.

Fish Curry

4 - 6 dessertspoons oil
4 cloves garlic, sliced
16 small red onions, sliced

Ground together without roasting:
3 dessertspoons ketumbar
(coriander)
2 dessertspoons jintan puteh
(cumin)
12 dried chillies, seeded
1 small piece turmeric
1 teaspoon peppercorns

1 or 2 sprigs curry leaves
About 2 cups of coconut milk
from ½ coconut
1 cup of tamarind juice,
or to taste
Salt
3 brinjals, cut into pieces and
to be left soaking in water
1 kati (21 oz, 600 g) ikan kurau
(threadfin), cut into pieces
½ teaspoon fresh ginger, sliced

Put oil in pan. Fry sliced garlic and onions till soft, but not brown. Add ground ingredients and curry leaves. Add coconut milk, tamarind and salt.

When boiling, add brinjals and, when nearly cooked, add fish. Allow to simmer till fish is cooked and oil rises to the top.

Note:
Brinjals can be left out.

Savory Prawns

1 kati (21 oz, 600 g) medium-sized fresh prawns

Ground together to a smooth paste:
6 fresh red chillies, seeded
2 buah keras (candlenuts)
1 piece dry turmeric, size of an almond

Salt to taste
6 dessertspoons oil

Remove heads and shells of prawns but leave tails on. Slit each prawn in two up to tail.

Mix ground ingredients and salt with prawns. Heat oil in pan and put all the prawns in. Fry till prawns are cooked for about 20 minutes, stirring once in a while.

Prawn Sothi

2½ teacups coconut milk (½ cup first squeeze, rest second squeeze) from ¾ coconut
½ teaspoon turmeric powder
Salt to taste
12 small red onions, sliced
2 fresh red and 2 fresh green chillies, coarsely sliced
½ kati (10½ oz, 300 g) fresh prawns, shelled and cleaned
2 sprigs curry leaves
Lime juice to taste

Put in pan 2 cups second squeeze coconut milk. Add turmeric and salt, onions and chillies and bring to boil. Add prawns and curry leaves.

When prawns are properly cooked, add the ½ cup first squeeze coconut milk and as much lime juice as you like. Stir the gravy gently to prevent gravy curdling until it boils. Remove from fire and serve.

For variety:
Use 300g fish (ikan kurau, threadfin) cut into small pieces in place of prawns.

Note:
This is a coconut milk dish to serve with a dry curry.

Mulligatawny Soup

2 dessertspoons oil
4 cloves garlic, bruised
½ teacup small onions,
  bruised
½ teaspoon alba (brown
  mustard seeds)

Ground together:
3 tablespoons ketumbar
  (coriander)
2 dessertspoons jintan puteh
  (cumin)
2 dessertspoon jintan manis
  (anise)
1 teaspoon peppercorns
6 dried chillies, seeded
1 piece turmeric
A very small piece of
  cinnamon
2 cloves
1 teaspoon mustard seed

1 chicken steamed, shredded,
  reserve bones
2 cups water
Salt
2 - 3 teacups coconut milk
  from ½ coconut
A little tamarind juice to
  taste
12 small onions, sliced and
  fried brown for garnishing
Boiled rice for garnishing

Put oil in deep pan and fry the garlic and onions. When golden brown, add alba and ground ingredients and fry a few minutes.

Add chicken bones and two cups of water and salt and allow to simmer for ½ hour.

Strain and return gravy to pan, add coconut milk and tamarind juice and a little more salt, if necessary. When boiling add shredded chicken.

Serve with fried onions. Add 1 tablespoon of boiled rice to each cup of soup.

Pepper Water

4 cloves garlic in skin,
  smashed
6 small onions in skin,
  smashed
2 dessertspoons oil
4 dried chillies, broken into
  pieces

Very coarsely ground together:
1 dessertspoon ketumbar
  (coriander)
1 teaspoon jintan puteh
  (cumin)
1 teaspoon peppercorns

4 teacups thin tamarind juice
Salt to taste

Fry smashed garlic and onions in oil till a little brown, add chillies, and fry just a little. Add tamarind juice mixed with ground spices and then salt. Boil for 20 minutes. Strain before serving.

Puri

1½ cups atta (whole wheat
  flour) or ordinary white
  flour
⅓ teaspoon salt
1½ level dessertspoons ghee
½ cup diluted evaporated
  milk to which juice of
  1 lime has been added to
  sour it
Ghee for frying puris

Sieve flour into basin, add salt. With a fork mix the ghee till you get the consistency of breadcrumbs. Now add the sour milk and with finger tips mix into a soft rollable dough and knead a little. Cover basin with damp cloth for 10 minutes.

Now break the dough into about 20 small portions. Roll each into a ball between your palms. Roll each out on the board, floured with whole wheat flour, to form a pancake about 7 cm in diameter.

Heat about 8 tablespoons ghee in a small kwali and fry the puris, one at a time, gently pressing down the puri with a flat spoon. When the puri floats and is slightly brown on one side, turn it over to brown it on the other side. Drain on absorbent paper.

Serve puris with any kind of curry, vegetable dish (page 196), dhall (page 200) and Pineapple and Apple Chutney (page 187).

Note:
Atta is obtainable at Indian grocery shops.

Note from this edition:
You may use buttermilk instead of evaporated milk with lime juice.

Puri with Fish Curry (page 209)

Yellow Rice

Fresh turmeric, size of an
  almond, ground to a paste
3 cups rice, washed and
  drained
4 cups coconut milk from
  1 large coconut, remove
  brown skin before grating
1½ teaspoons salt
4 cloves
Small piece of cinnamon
Fried onions
Shredded omelette

Put ground turmeric in 1 dessertspoon of water and
strain through very fine muslin. Add the yellow liquid
to the coconut milk.

Put rice, coconut milk and salt in a deep pan and
cook as you would ordinary rice. When liquid has
been absorbed, stir, add cloves and cinnamon. Cover
pan and leave on very slow fire till properly cooked.

Put rice on platter, decorate with fried onions and
shredded omelette.

Note:
If you like the flavour of pandan, shred 2 pandan
leaves and add to rice and coconut milk before
boiling.

Pilau

4 tablespoons butter or ghee
2 cloves garlic, sliced
1 large or 12 small onions,
  sliced
¼ teaspoon ginger, sliced
4 teaspoons rice, washed and
  drained
5 teacups water (more if
  necessary)
Salt to taste
1 teacup milk
20 almonds blanched
1 in (2½ cm) cube fresh
  coconut, finely ground
A small piece cinnamon
4 cardamons
4 cloves
2 bundles coriander leaves
Fried onions
Shredded omelette or slices
  of hard boiled egg

Put butter or ghee in deep pan. Fry garlic till brown,
then add onions. When slightly brown add ginger
and rice. Fry a little. Then add 5 teacups water and
salt. Cover pan and allow to boil till water has been
absorbed.

Add the milk into which the ground almonds and
coconut have been mixed, stirring well. Add spices
and coriander leaves. Replace cover and allow to
cook on very slow fire.

Garnish with fried onions and shredded omelette of
sliced hard boiled egg.

Note:
Serve with chicken or beef curry.

Chicken Pilau

1 chicken (1½ lb, 680 g)
2 large onions, diced
1 sprig celery
3 tablespoons butter or ghee
  (less if chicken is very fat)
1 clove garlic, chopped finely
¼ teaspoon finely chopped
  ginger
2½ teacups rice, washed and
  drained
5 teacups chicken stock
20 blanched almonds, finely
  ground
Cinnamon, cloves,
  cardamons for flavouring
3 tablespoons raisins
Fried onions

Boil chicken in water to which a little salt, 2 dessertspoons of the diced onions and sprig of celery have been added. Do not overcook chicken. Remove chicken on a plate and keep both chicken and stock for use later.

Put in a deep pan the butter or ghee. When hot put in garlic and when a little browned, add the rest of the diced onions. When golden brown, add ginger and the whole chicken.

Cook till evenly browned, then add the rice and stock, in which the ground almonds have been mixed. Cover pan and allow to simmer slowly.

When rice is nearly dry add spices, raisins, more salt if necessary, and stir well. Simmer till rice is properly cooked.

To serve:
Cut up chicken into pieces. Spread the rice and chicken on large platter. And decorate top with fried onions. Serve with meat curry and chutney or pickle.

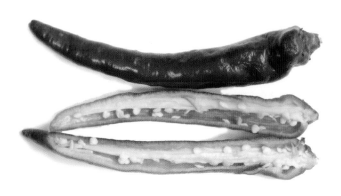

Briani

CURRIED MEAT:
2 kati (2½ lb, 1.2 kg) mutton,
   beef or chicken
½ teaspoon fresh ginger,
   ground
4 - 5 tablespoons tinned ghee
   or butter
2 large onions, diced
Cinnamon, cardamon and
   cloves for flavouring

Ground together:
4 tablespoons ketumbar
   (coriander)
1½ teaspoons jintan puteh
   (cumin)
1½ teaspoons jintan manis
   (anise)
1½ teaspoons white
   peppercorns
1 tablespoon kas-kas
   (if mutton is used)

Salt
Water, as much as is required
2 teacups evaporated milk
   curdled with juice of one
   lime (½ cup milk to 1½ cups
   of water)

RICE:
4 tablespoons or more ghee
4 cloves garlic, ground
12 small onions, ground
A little ginger, ground
4 cups good rice, washed and
   drained
4½ cups water
1 teacup evaporated milk
   curdled with juice of 1 lime
20 almonds, ground to a fine
   paste
2 bundles of coriander leaves

For meat:
Cut meat into pieces and rub over with ginger.

Put ghee in pan, add onions and fry till slightly browned. Add cinnamon, cardamon and cloves and ground curry paste. Add meat and salt and fry for a few minutes.

Add a little water and boil till meat is a little tender. Add curdled milk. Cook till the curry is quite thick.

For rice:
Put ghee in cooking pot, brown garlic, then add onions, and then ginger. Add rice and fry a few minutes.

Add water and then the milk in which almond paste has been mixed. Add salt and stir thoroughly. Cover pan and boil.

When rice has absorbed the water and milk, put the curried meat and coriander leaves into a hollow made in the rice. Cover curried meat with rice and leave on very slow fire to cook very slowly till time to serve. Mix well before serving.

Serve with:
Curry (beef or chicken).
Sliced cucumber, tomatoes and pineapple mixed with tomato sauce or chilli sauce.
Indian pickle or chutney.

Notes from this edition:
Add a pinch of saffron to give the briani a rich colour and taste.

You may use buttermilk instead of evaporated milk with lime juice.

Khichree

3 tablespoons butter or ghee
1 large onion, diced
2½ cups rice, washed and
   drained
½ cup lentils, washed, soaked
   in water and drained
1 slice of ginger
2 in (5 cm) piece of cinnamon
4 cloves
Salt to taste
4½ cups (about) water
Fried onions

Put in deep pan ghee or butter. Fry diced onions till brown. Add rice and lentils and stir till all fat has been absorbed. Add ginger and spices, salt and water.

Cover pan and simmer till water has been completely absorbed. Stir occasionally to prevent burning.

To serve, place khichree on large platter and sprinkle fried onions on the top.

Serve with meat curry, chutney and Indian pickle.

Fish Kedgeree

1 lb (450 g) fish, sliced in 1 in
   (2½ cm) thickness
4 cups cooked rice, must be
   hot
4 dessertspoons butter
Salt and pepper
3 coddled eggs
Potato crisps
Sprigs of parsley

Fry the pieces of fish till brown on the outside but soft inside. Debone and flake.

When all ingredients are ready for mixing, put in large platter 2 or 3 tablespoons of rice. Quickly mix in a little butter, salt and pepper, then break an egg and stir it into the rice. Repeat process till all rice, butter and eggs are used up.

Spread rice evenly on platter and spread the flaked fish on top. Surround with potato crisps and garnish with sprigs of parsley.

Serve with meat curry, pickle and chutney such as Fresh Tomato Chutney (page 53).

Note:
Use ikan kurau (threadfin) or ikan tenggiri (mackerel).

Note from this edition:
To coddle eggs, pierce large end of egg with a pin. Put cold water with 1½ teaspoon salt in saucepan. Submerge eggs in one layer and simmer on medium heat. Remove from heat, cover and leave for 4-6 minutes depending on how well cooked the yolk is desired. Halt cooking by running under cold water.

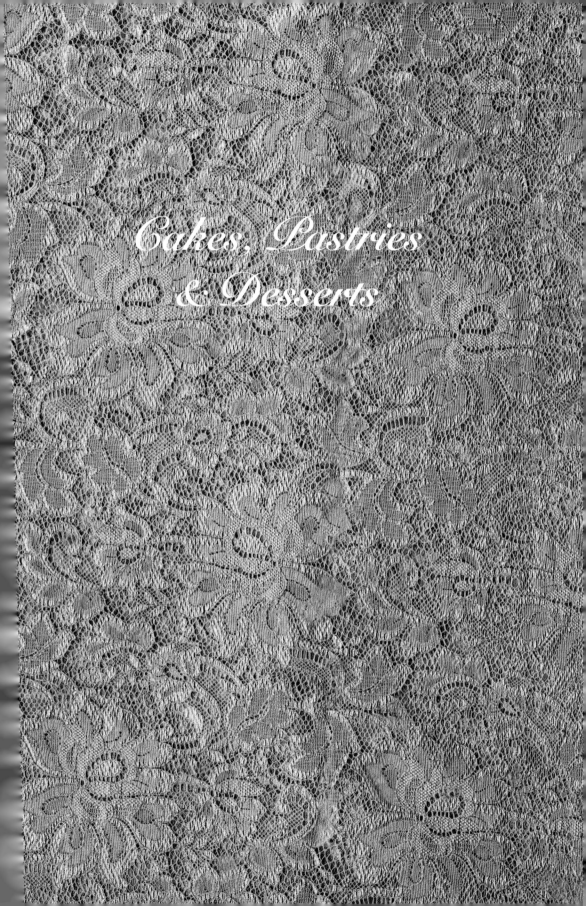

Cakes, Pastries & Desserts

Not Very Rich Cup Cakes

4 oz (115 g) butter
½ cup sugar
2 eggs, yolks to be separated
   from whites
⅓ cup of orange juice
Grated rind of ½ orange
1½ cups self-raising flour or
   1½ cups flour sifted with
   1½ teaspoons baking powder

Cream butter, add sugar and beat until light and creamy. Add egg yolks, one by one, and beat well.

Add grated rind of ½ orange. Add egg whites which have been beaten to a stiff froth, folding it in. Add flour, a little at a time, folding in until mixture is smooth. Add orange juice.

When well mixed, put batter into greased and floured cake cups. Bake in moderate oven for 20-25 minutes.

Note:
If orange rind is to be used, scrape the rind off on a grater before the orange is cut into two.

Variations:
Leave out rind if you do not care for the flavour but use the orange juice. For a stronger orange flavour, use 1½ tablespoons grated rind.

Milk can be used instead orange juice. With milk use ½ teaspoon vanilla.

Rich Pound Cake

8 oz (225 g) butter
8 oz (225 g) fine sugar, less if
   desired
6 eggs, yolks to be separated
   from whites
1 teaspoon vanilla
8 oz (225 g) flour sifted twice
   with 2 teaspoons baking
   powder or 8 oz (225 g) self-
   raising flour sifted twice

Cream butter, add sugar and beat until light and creamy. Add egg yolks, one by one, and beat well.

Add vanilla then fold in egg whites which have been beaten to a stiff froth. Add flour, a little at a time, folding in until mixture is smooth.

When well mixed, put batter into small greased sandwich tin which has been lined and greased. Bake in moderate oven for 20-25 minutes.

Note:
If an orange flavour is required, leave out vanilla. Use grated rind of ½ orange and about 2 tablespoons orange juice.

Orange Cake (1)

7 oz (200 g) butter
7 oz (200 g) sugar
6 eggs, yolks separated from
   whites
8 oz (225 g) self-raising flour
   or 8 oz (225 g) flour sifted
   with 2 teaspoons baking
   powder
Juice of ½ orange
   (three tablespoons)
1 teaspoon vanilla or grated
   rind of ½ orange
A little cochineal

Cream butter and sugar till light. Add yolks of eggs, one at a time, beating well after addition of each egg. When light add the egg whites which have been beaten to a stiff froth, folding it in.

Add flour, folding it in, and when mixture is smooth, add vanilla or orange juice and rind.

Pour half of the mixture into a square or round deep cake tin which has been lined and greased. Then add a little cochineal to remaining mixture to make a pretty pink.

Pour mixture on to that in tin. Bake in moderately hot oven for about 1 hour or till cake leaves sides of pan.

When cool cover cake with fudge frosting (see page 251).

Orange Cake (2)

4 oz (115 g) butter
4 oz (115 g) sugar
3 eggs, yolks separated from
   whites
Grated rind of ½ orange
6 oz (170 g) self raising flour
   or 6 oz (170 g) ordinary flour
   sifted with 1½ teaspoons
   baking powder
Juice of ½ orange
   (three tablespoons)

Cream butter and sugar. Add egg yolks, one at a time, and beat well. Add grated rind.

Add egg whites which have been beaten to a stiff froth. Add in flour, folding it in, till smooth. Add orange juice. Pour batter into two sandwich tins which have been greased and lined.

Bake for about ½ hour in moderate oven. When done, remove cake from oven and cool on cake rack. Spread butter icing (see below) between layers and on top and sprinkle over it coloured sugar drops, chopped walnuts, or grated chocolate.

To make Butter Icing:
Beat together 2 tablespoons butter and 3 tablespoons icing sugar.

Sponge Sandwich with Orange Cream Filling

CAKE:

3 eggs, yolks separated
  from whites
3 oz (85 g) fine sugar
2 tablespoons boiling water
¼ -½ teaspoon vanilla
3 oz (85 g) flour sifted with
  ¼ teaspoon baking powder
Pinch of salt
Icing sugar

ORANGE CREAM FILLING:

¼ cup fresh orange juice
½ cup milk
2½ level dessertspoons
  custard powder
2 level dessertspoons sugar
1 dessertspoon butter

To make cake:
Prepare oven, grease sandwich tins and line bottom with greased paper.

Whisk egg whites till fluffy. In a separate bowl, add egg yolks one at a time, and beat for a few minutes. Add sugar and beat for about 10 minutes till thick and creamy.

Add boiling water and beat for another 5 minutes. Add vanilla. Add flour which has been sifted with baking powder and salt, folding it gradually into the egg mixture, using a spoon or the whisk. Fold in the fluffy egg whites into the batter.

Pour mixture into tins and bake in a quick oven for ten minutes till set and golden brown.

Turn the cake quickly on to sugared paper. Remove greased paper from cake, spread with hot jam or orange cream filling and place one cake on the other to from a sandwich. Sprinkle icing sugar on top.

To make orange cream filling:
Mix all ingredients, except butter, in enamel pan and cook on slow fire, stirring all the time till mixture thickens and boils.

Add butter, remove from fire, allow to cool and then use as filling for sponge sandwich, or Choux Pastry shells (see page234).

Variation:
To make Chocolate Sponge Sandwich, use 1¾ oz (50 g) flour and 1¼ oz (35 g) cocoa.

Coffee Cake

8 oz (225 g) butter
6 oz (170 g) castor sugar
4 large eggs
4 heaping teaspoons instant
coffee
8 oz (225 g) self-raising flour
1 teaspoon vanilla
1 tablespoon brandy

Cream butter, add sugar and beat till fluffy. Add eggs, one at a time, then instant coffee. Add flour, a little at a time, and continue beating, adding vanilla and brandy before the last addition of flour is mixed in.

Pour mixture into greased cake tin, with bottom lined with brown paper. Bake for 1 hour 10 minutes at 190°C.

For variety:
Add 2 teaspoons cinnamon powder if you like the flavour.

Banana Cake

8 oz (225 g) flour
1 teaspoon baking powder
1 teaspoon bicarbonate
of soda
6 oz (170 g) butter
6 oz (170 g) sugar
2 eggs
2 tablespoons milk
1 cup mashed ripe banana,
about 3 large pisang hijau

Sift together the flour, baking powder and bicarbonate of soda.

Cream butter and sugar. Add the eggs, one at a time, and beat well. Add the milk and the banana. Add the flour which has been sifted with baking powder and bicarbonate of soda.

Bake in moderate oven for about 1 hour.

Banana Orange Cake

6 oz (170 g) sugar
6 oz (170 g) butter
4 eggs, yolks separated from
whites
1 cup mashed ripe bananas,
about 3 large pisang hijau
8 oz (225 g) self-raising flour,
sifted with ¾ teaspoon
bicarbonate of soda
3 tablespoons orange juice

Cream butter and sugar till light. Add egg yolks, one at a time, and continue beating. Then add mashed banana. Beat well.

Fold in the egg whites which have been whisked to a stiff froth. Fold in the flour, and last of all the orange juice.

Bake in greased cake tin at 350°F (175°C) for about an hour.

Chocolate Cake

6 oz (170 g) flour
2 teaspoons baking powder
2 oz (55 g) cocoa
A pinch of salt
7 oz (200 g) butter
7 oz (200 g) sugar
6 eggs, yolks separated
  from whites
2 teaspoons vanilla
1 dessertspoon brandy

Sift together flour, baking powder, cocoa and salt.

Cream butter and sugar till very light. Add egg yolks, one at a time, beating well after each addition.

Add egg whites which have been whipped to a stiff froth. Add vanilla and brandy and then fold in the flour which has been sifted with baking powder and cocoa.

Bake in a greased and lined tin in a moderate oven for an hour or till cake leaves sides of tin.

Note:
For richer cake use 8 oz (225 g) butter.

Chocolate Cinnamon Cake

8 oz (225 g) butter
6 oz (170 g) castor sugar
4 large eggs

Sifted together:
7 oz (200 g) self-raising flour
1 oz (30 g) dark cocoa powder
2 teaspoons powdered
  cinnamon
½ teaspoon baking powder

1 teaspoon vanilla
1 tablespoon brandy

Cream butter, add sugar and beat until fluffy. Add eggs, one at a time, beating well after each addition.

Add the flour mixture a little at a time, and continue beating, adding vanilla and then brandy before the last addition of flour is mixed in.

Pour mixture into a cake tin, greased and with bottom lined with brown paper. Bake for 1 hour and 10 minutes at 375°F (190°C).

Note:
A non-stick cake tin is useful.

Swiss Roll

3 eggs, yolks separated
  from whites
3 oz (85 g) fine sugar
2 tablespoons boiling water
3 oz (85 g) flour sifted with
  ¼ teaspoon baking powder
Pinch of salt
¼-½ teaspoon vanilla

Prepare oven, grease sandwich tins and line bottom with greased paper.

Whisk egg whites till fluffy. In a separate bwol, add egg yolks one at a time, and beat for a few minutes. Add sugar and beat for about 10 minutes till thick and creamy.

Add boiling water and beat for another 5 minutes. Add vanilla. Add flour which has been sifted with baking powder and salt, folding it gradually into the egg mixture, using a spoon or the whisk.Fold in the fluffy egg whites into the batter.

Pour mixture into a Swiss Roll tin and bake in a quick oven for ten minutes till set and golden brown.

When baked, turn cake quickly on to sugared paper, which should have underneath it, a damp cloth. Remove greased paper from cake, spread with hot jam and roll up quickly.

Cover with sugared paper and damp cloth for a little while to prevent the roll from cracking.

Cream Puffs

PUFFS:
1 cup boiling water
4 level dessertspoons butter
1 cup flour, sifted
Pinch of salt
3 eggs
2 teaspoons baking powder

FILLING:
1 heaping teaspoon flour
1 heaping teaspoon custard
  powder
1 cup milk
1 egg yolk, beaten
½ cup sugar, or less to taste
½ teaspoon vanilla

ECONOMICAL FILLING:
1 cup cold milk
4 teaspoons sugar
4 rounded teaspoons custard
  powder
½ teaspoon vanilla

To make Choux Pastry shells:
Put boiling water and butter into saucepan and boil. Add sifted flour and salt, stirring in well, till mixture is smooth and leaves sides of pan. Remove from fire and leave to cool a little.

Add eggs, one at a time. Beating well till smooth. Add baking powder and continue beating till air bubbles begin to appear in the mixture. Arrange in small heaps on greased baking tin, using two teaspoons.

Bake at moderately hot oven, 450°F (230°C), for about 40 minutes. When cool make slits at sides and fill with custard.

To make filling:
Mix flour and custard powder to thin paste with some milk. Add the beaten egg yolk.

Boil rest of milk with sugar. Then add flour paste, and stir well till it thickens. Add vanilla.

To make economical filling:
Boil milk and sugar. Add custard powder that has been made into a thin paste with some of the milk. When mixture thickens and boils, add vanilla.

Note:
For Orange Cream Filling, see filling for Sponge Sandwich (page 228).

Kiwa's Creole Loaf Cake

2 eggs
1 cup sugar
½ cup milk
1⅓ cups flour
1¾ teaspoons baking powder
¼ teaspoon salt
3 tablespoons melted butter
1 teaspoon vanilla

Cream eggs and sugar till very light and fluffy. Gradually beat in the milk. Then fold in the sifted flour, baking powder and salt. Add the butter. Flavour with 1 teaspoon vanilla.

Pour in greased and lined tin and bake in a moderate oven for about 50 minutes.

Spread top with Coffee Butter Icing (see below).

Coffee Butter Icing

1 tablespoon butter
2 tablespoons icing sugar
1-2 tablespoons cold, strong coffee or 1 teaspoon instant coffee
¼ - ½ teaspoon vanilla essence

Cream butter and sugar. Add coffee, a little at a time, beating constantly till light and fluffy. Add vanilla for flavouring.

Spread over cake after cake cools.

Sugee Cake

10 oz (280 g) butter
10 oz (280 g) sugar
4 oz (120 ml) milk
½ lb (225 g) semolina
13 eggs, yolks separated from whites
¼ lb (115 g) ground almonds
2 oz (55 g) flour
½ teaspoon bicarbonate of soda
1 dessertspoon brandy
2 teaspoons vanilla

Cream butter and three-quarters of sugar till light. Gradually add in the milk, beat all the time. Add semolina. Stir well and let it stand for 1 hour.

Add egg yolks which have been beaten with remainder of sugar, a little at a time.

Add whipped whites of 4 eggs and then almonds and flour sifted with bicarbonate of soda. Add brandy and vanilla.

Bake in moderate oven for about an hour.

Durian Cake

6 oz (170 g) butter
5 oz (140 g) sugar
4 eggs, yolks separated from whites
4 oz (115 g) durian meat, mashed
6 oz (170 g) self-raising flour

Beat butter and sugar till light. Add egg yolks, one at a time, beating well after each addition. Beat in the durian meat.

Fold in egg whites which have been beaten to a stiff froth. Fold in the flour.

Bake in greased tin for about an hour, at 350°F (175°C).

Rich Fruit Cake

¾ lb (340 g) butter or more if you like a richer cake
½ lb (225 g) sugar
12 eggs, yolks separated from whites
1 lb (455 g) flour
½ cup of grape juice
2 teaspoons cinnamon powder
4 - 5 dessertspoons treacle or golden syrup or some of each
2 tablespoons brandy

1 lb (455 g) raisins
¾ lb (340 g) sultanas
1 lb (455 g) currants
¼ lb (115 g) preserved ginger
½ lb (225 g) candied orange and lemon peel
¼ lb (115 g) candied cherries
¼ lb (115 g) dried figs
¼ lb (115 g) chopped almonds

Lightly cover the fruit and nut mixture with some of the 455g of flour. Reserve the rest of the flour for the cake mixture.

Cream butter and add sugar gradually. Separate yolks from whites of eggs and beat yolks till lemon coloured. Add beaten yolks to the creamed butter and sugar. Then add golden syrup and ground cinnamon.

Beat egg whites until stiff and add to yolk mixture. Then add the rest of the flour to the egg mixture. Add the grape juice and the brandy followed by the flour-covered fruit, a little at a time, mixing well.

Grease and line 3 medium-sized loaf tins. Bake in the oven at 150° C for about 90 minutes till done.

Remove from oven. Leave cakes in tins for 30 minutes before turning them out on to a wire rack to cool. Wrap cakes in tin foil. Keep for at least 3-4 days before serving.

Gingerbread

2 cups flour
½ teaspoon salt
1 teaspoon baking powder
1 teaspoon bicarbonate
  of soda
2 teaspoons ground ginger
½ teaspoon ground cloves or
  nutmeg
1 teaspoon cinnamon powder
¼ cup (2 oz, 60 g) butter
½ cup sugar
½ cup treacle or golden syrup
  or ¼ cup of each
2 eggs
⅓ cup of boiling water

Sift all dry ingredients, including spices.

Cream butter and sugar. Add treacle and beat well. Reserve.

Beat eggs and add the hot water, then the reserved creamed mixture.

Stir in dry ingredients gradually. Beat well. Pour in greased and lined tin and bake in moderate oven for 30-40 minutes till firm.

Notes:
Add ¼ cup sliced preserved ginger to mixture, if you like, after flour has been mixed in.

Gula melaka syrup (see page 279) can be used instead of treacle.

Mushroom Cake

3 oz (85 g) flour
3 oz (85 g) cornflour or
  custard powder
1½ level teaspoons baking
  powder
4 oz (115 g) butter or margarine
4 oz (115 g) sugar
3 eggs
A little milk, if necessary

Sift flour, cornflour and baking powder.

Cream butter and sugar. Add eggs, one by one, and beat well. Add flour mixture gradually and, if necessary, a little milk, to make a creamy texture.

Half fill greased buns tin. Bake 15-20 minutes in moderate oven.

When cool, cut out centres with a small pasty cutter or knife two-thirds of the way down. Fill the hollow with jam or cream or both. Then put cut-out piece on top and sprinkle with icing sugar.

Kwa's Mocha Tart

5 eggs
Pinch of salt
Pinch of baking powder
1 cup sugar
2 tablespoons coffee essence
1 cup flour sifted with
  1 teaspoon baking powder
Almonds for garnishing

Separate the eggs. Whisk whites with salt and pinch of baking powder. When stiff, add in egg yolks one at a time. Add sugar gradually, beating all the time. Beat in coffee essence. Fold in flour.

Bake in two well-greased and lined 9 in (23 cm) sandwich tins in moderate oven for half an hour. Cool.

Spread Coffee Butter Icing (see page 235) between layers and on top of cake. Sprinkle top with browned almonds which have been finely shredded.

Russell's Swiss Apricot Tart

SHORT CRUST:
3 oz (85 g) butter
6 oz (170 g) flour
Pinch of salt
¾ teaspoon baking powder
1 egg

FILLING:
4 tablespoons butter
4 tablespoons sugar
4 eggs, yolks separated from
  whites
3 level tablespoons flour
¼ teaspoon baking powder
1 large tin apricots, well
  drained

To make short crust:
Rub butter into flour which has been sifted with salt and baking powder. Add beaten egg and a little water to make a soft dough. Roll, and line round cake tin with a short crust and bake lightly in moderate oven.

To make filling:
Cream butter and sugar. Add egg yolks one at a time and beat well. Add flour which has been sifted with the baking powder. Add apricots and mix well.

To make tart:
Fill the baked pie crust with the above mixture and bake for ¾ hour in a moderate oven.

Beat the egg whites to a stiff froth with 2 dessertspoons sugar. When pie is cool, spread the whites over the top and bake in cool oven.

Date Rolls

Sifted together:
4 oz (115 g) plain flour
4 oz (115 g) self-raising flour

5 oz (140 g) butter or
margarine
1 egg, beaten with enough
milk to mix dough to a
rollable consistency.
½ lb (225 g) seedless dates,
remove skin if tough

Keep a little egg and milk mixture for brushing tops of date rolls.

Put flour mixture in basin and with a fork or fingers mix the butter into it to get the consistency of breadcrumbs. Add egg and milk mixture to form a rollable dough.

Break dough into 4 parts. Shape each so that when rolled it will form a rectangle. Roll out to thickness of ¼ in (½ cm). Cut into pieces 2¼ x 1¼ in (5½ x 3 cm). Put a date in each width-ways, fold one end over the other.

Place rolls in greased baking sheet, folded side on it. When all the rolls are made, press fork on top rolls to make grooves.

Brush with egg and milk mixture, and bake at 400°F (200°C) for 30 minutes or till golden brown.

Current / Raisin Loaf

1 oz (30 g) fresh yeast
2 tablespoons flour
2 tablespoons sugar
4 tablespoons lukewarm
  water
¼ cup sweetened condensed
  milk
2 tablespoons butter
1½ teaspoons salt
¼ cup boiling water
1½ cups lukewarm water
2 egg yolks, beaten
6 cups sifted flour
Extra flour for dusting work
  surface
1½ cups mixed fruit:
  currants, raisins, sultanas,
  mixed peel, glace fruit
Egg white and ½ teaspoon
  milk for brushing top of
  loaves

Prepare yeast with flour, sugar and lukewarm water. Put all these ingredients into a small basin and mix till smooth. Leave in a warm place to rise. (The plate rack of a gas store is a good place).

Put in a large enamel saucepan the condensed milk, butter, salt and boiling water. Stir well. Then add the 1½ cups lukewarm water. Stir in the beaten egg yolks.

Put into large porcelain bowl 6 cups of flour. Make a well in the centre and pour in all the yeast preparation and the milk preparation a little at a time, mixing the flour gradually into the liquid.

When all liquid has been used up and all the mixture is smooth, toss on floured board and knead, adding as much flour as is necessary to make a soft elastic dough. (At this stage dough should not stick to fingers).

Return dough to bowl, pressing it down with fingers on which a little butter has been rubbed. Cover bowl with a clean cloth and leave in a warm place to rise until mixture has doubled its bulk.

Turn dough on to floured board again and knead, mixing in the fruit.

Then cut into three equal parts, putting each down into a greased tin and patting down so that dough has an even surface and reaches halfway up the tin.

Return to warm place to allow dough to rise again until mixture has doubled its bulk.

Brush top of loaves with white of egg beaten slightly with a few drops of milk. Bake in hot oven for 40 minutes or until done.

Kwa's Speculaas

½ cup (4 oz , 115 g) butter
½ cup (4 oz , 115 g) brown
  sugar
2 eggs
1 tablespoon milk
2½ teaspoons cinnamon
  powder
1½ teaspoons ground cloves
1½ teaspoon ground nutmeg
½ teaspoon bicarbonate
  of soda
2-3 cups flour
5 drops of lemon essence

Cream butter and sugar. Beat in eggs and milk. Add spices, bicarbonate of soda, lemon essence and enough flour to make a rollable dough. Roll out thin, about 3mm, cut into pieces and bake in moderate oven for 10-15 minutes.

Coconut Cookies

4 oz (115 g) butter
½ cup sugar
2 eggs
4 oz (115 g) dessicated
  coconut
½ teaspoon vanilla
6 oz (170 g) self-raising flour

Beat butter and sugar to a cream. Add eggs, one at a time, and then dessicated coconut and vanilla. Stir in the flour well.

Drop on cold greased baking sheets, ½ dessertspoon at a time leaving room for cookies to spread, and bake in slow oven for 30 minutes.

Kwa's Coconut Cookies

4 oz (115 g) butter
½ cup sugar
2 eggs
3 oz (85 g) dessicated coconut
2-3 cups flour
½ teaspoon vanilla
Caster sugar and dessicated
  coconut for decorating

Cream butter and sugar. Beat in eggs. Add coconut. Add enough flour to make rollable dough. Roll out thin. Cut into pieces. Decorate top with caster sugar and dessicated coconut and bake in moderate oven for 10 – 15 minutes.

Sophia Blackmore's Jam Drops

1½ tablespoons butter
¼ cup sugar
1 egg
½ teaspoon vanilla essence
1¼ cups self-raising flour or
   1¼ cups flour and 1¼
   teaspoons baking powder
Some jam

Beat butter and sugar to a cream. Add egg and vanilla essence and beat well. Add flour and mix well. Form into 16 balls with fingers, using flour to enable easy handling.

Take each ball, make hole in centre with finger, fill with jam and make into balls again.

Place on greased baking pan and bake in moderate oven for 15 minutes.

Note:
These Jam Drops have the texture of biscuits.

Coconut Biscuits

½ coconut
4 oz (115 g) butter
4 oz (115 g) sugar
1 egg

Sifted together:
3 oz (85 g) self-raising flour
3 oz (85 g) plain flour
3 oz (85 g) cornflour

Remove brown skin from coconut before grating. Roast grated coconut to golden brown in moderate oven, stirring coconut occasionally. This should give you one cup.

Beat together butter and sugar till fluffy. Add egg and beat well. Add the sifted flour mixture and, when smooth, add the roasted coconut. Mix well.

Press dough through biscuit presser with rather large holes (because of the coconut) to make the patterns you desire onto greased baking sheets.

Alternatively, for easy work, put teaspoon lumps of dough on greased baking sheets and press the tops down with a small fork to make grooves on surface.

Bake at 350°F (175°C) for about 30 minutes or till golden brown.

Kwa's Peanut Butter Cookies

55 g (2 oz) butter
½ cup sugar
170 g (6 oz) peanut butter
2 eggs
3 tablespoons milk
2 cups flour sifted with
   2 teaspoons baking powder
Chopped peanuts for
   decorating

Cream butter and sugar and then add peanut butter. Beat in the eggs, one at a time and then beat in the milk. Mix in the flour.

Drop from tip of teaspoon on to buttered baking sheet. Flatten slightly. Decorate with chopped peanuts. Bake in slow oven for 10-15 minutes.

Peanut Butter Cookies

4 oz (115 g) butter
4 oz (115 g) sugar
1 egg
4 oz (115 g) peanut butter,
   creamy or crunchy

Sifted together:
4 oz (115 g) plain flour
4 oz (115 g) self-raising flour
2 oz (55 g) cornflour

Cream butter and sugar. Add egg and then the peanut butter. Add flour mixture and mix well.

If creamy peanut butter is used, press batter through cookie-presser onto greased baking sheets. If crunchy peanut butter is used, then using teaspoon, put $^{3}/_{4}$ teaspoon lumps of batter on baking sheets and press top of each with tines of fork to make a little design.

Bake at 350°F (175°C) for about 40 minutes.

Kwa's Ginger Cookies

4 oz (115 g) butter
½ cup brown sugar
2 tablespoons golden syrup
   or treacle
3 tablespoons syrup from
   Canton preserved ginger
2 eggs
2½ cups flour sifted with
   ½ teaspoon bicarbonate
   of soda
2 teaspoon ground ginger
1 teaspoon ground cinnamon
Canton ginger for decorating

Cream butter and sugar. Beat in treacle and ginger syrup. Beat in the eggs, one in a time. Mix in the dry ingredients. Drop by teaspoonful on to buttered baking sheet. Flatten slightly and decorate top with strips of Canton ginger. Bake in slow oven for 10 – 15 minutes.

Pancakes

4 oz (115 g) flour
1 teaspoon baking powder
Pinch of salt
2 eggs, beaten
½ pint (240 ml) milk
Butter for frying
Juice from 4 limes

Sift flour, baking powder and salt into basin. Add beaten eggs and about half of the milk. Beat well till smooth. Add rest of milk and leave to stand for a while.

Grease bottom of frying pan with butter. Pour in quickly enough batter to cover the bottom of pan, fry till golden brown on under side, turn and fry on second side.

Turn on to sugared paper, spread with jam or sprinkle with sugar and lime juice. Then roll up and serve.

Banana Pancakes

2 eggs
½ cup water or milk
1 cup self-raising or 1 cup
    flour sifted with 1 teaspoon
    baking powder
6 bananas (pisang rajah),
    mashed
2 dessertspoons sugar
Pinch of salt
Oil for frying
Juice from 4 limes

Beat eggs till light, add milk or water, and stir into flour till smooth. Add mashed banana and sugar and salt.

Fry in hot oil, not deep, turning pancakes when one side browns. When golden brown, remove, drain on paper.

Place on platter, sprinkle sugar and a few drops of lime juice on pancakes.

Waffles

2 cups flour
3 teaspoons baking powder
½ teaspoon salt
2 eggs, separated
1¾ cups milk
2 tablespoons melted butter

Sift together dry ingredients, add slightly beaten egg yolks and milk; beat thoroughly. Add melted butter and fold in stiffly beaten egg whites. Bake in hot waffle iron until brown.

Serve with butter and gula melaka syrup or Golden Syrup.

Scones

2 tablespoons butter or
  margarine
2 cups flour
2 eggs, well beaten
½ cup milk
3 teaspoons baking powder

Sift flour and baking powder together twice.

Rub fat into flour lightly with fingers till flour and butter look like breadcrumbs. Avoid making an oily mixture.

Add eggs and milk, which have been beaten together, to make soft dough.

Place dough on floured baking pan, flatten top to make a round shape, ½ in (about 1.2 cm) thick. Cut with floured knife into eight sections.

Brush top with left over milk and egg. Bake in hot oven for 15-20 minutes.

Serve with butter and jam after separating pieces.

Notes:
If using self-raising flour, omit baking powder.

For scones without eggs, use about ½ cup milk to which 1 dessertspoon lime juice or vinegar has been added to sour it.

Note from this edition:
To make small scones, cut the dough with a 6 cm (2.5 in) round cutter.

Drop Scones

1½ cups self-raising flour
  or 1½ cups flour sifted with
  1½ teaspoons baking
  powder
½ teaspoon salt
2 eggs
1 cup milk
Butter for greasing pan

Mix in a bowl all dry ingredients. Make a well in centre, put in the eggs, mix and beat in the flour, a little at a time, adding the milk gradually. Beat until smooth.

Heat heavy frying pan or electric hot plate. Grease with butter. Drop batter by tablespoons on to pan. Turn quickly when bubbles appear. Brown on each side. Serve with butter and jam or Golden Syrup.

Custard

½ cup milk
½ cup water
3 dessertspoons sugar
2 teaspoons vanilla-flavoured
   custard powder
A pinch of salt
¼ teaspoon vanilla

Mix the milk, water, sugar and custard powder together and boil in a small enamel pan, stirring all the time to prevent burning and to keep custard smooth. When mixture boils, add salt and vanilla, and pour into jug.

Orange Custard

½ cup orange juice
½ cup evaporated milk
3 dessertspoons sugar,
   or to taste
2 teaspoons custard powder

Mix the juice, milk, sugar and custard powder together and boil in a small enamel pan, stirring all the time to prevent burning and to keep custard smooth. Pour into jug to serve.

Baked Custard

2 eggs
3 tablespoons sugar
¾ cup evaporated milk
   diluted with ¾ water
¼ teaspoon salt
¼ teaspoon vanilla essence
1 dessertspoon butter

Beat eggs till light, add sugar and continue beating to dissolve it. Add milk, salt and vanilla.

Grease small Pyrex dish, pour mixture in, put dabs of butter on top and bake in slow oven till custard sets.

Variation – Baked Caramel Custard:
Put 2 level tablespoons sugar in pan and place over small flame to dissolve and brown it. Stir sugar till it dissolves and takes on a light brown colour. (Do not burn the sugar).

Pour the caramel into a Pyrex dish. Make custard mixture according to recipe given, reducing sugar to 1½ tablespoons, and pour it over the caramel. Bake in slow oven until set. Allow to cool before turning out.

Fudge

3 cups sugar
3 dessertspoons cocoa
3 dessertspoons golden syrup
1 cup evaporated milk
Pinch of salt
2 dessertspoons butter
1 teaspoon vanilla
¼ teaspoon baking powder
1 cup chopped walnuts and/
  or ¼ cup chopped
  preserved ginger

Put in deep pan sugar, cocoa, golden syrup, milk and salt. Stir well with wooden spoon and place pan on very small fire. Do not stir before sugar dissolves, but with the spoon gently move sugar at the bottom of the pan once in a while to prevent burning.

When mixture begins to boil, stir, add butter and keep stirring. Increase flame a little till mixture thickens. When tiny bubbles appear on edge of spoon and at the bottom of pan as you stir, test drops of fudge in a cup of cold water, and if they form soft balls in your fingers, add vanilla and baking powder.

Remove pan from fire. After five minutes of cooling beat mixture till it begins to harden. Add walnuts and/or ginger and quickly pour on to greased square tin. When cool cut into squares and size you like.

Variation:
If you like a darker fudge, add more cocoa. If you like a lighter fudge, add less cocoa.

Fudge Frosting

2 cups sugar
2 tablespoons golden syrup
3 tablespoons cocoa
½ cup evaporated milk
A pinch of salt
2 tablespoons butter
½ teaspoon baking powder
1 teaspoon vanilla essence

Cook sugar, golden syrup, cocoa and milk and salt on very small fire till sugar is dissolved, stirring a little now and then to prevent burning. When sugar is dissolved and mixture is boiling, increase heat, stirring all the time.

When mixture begins to thicken, place a drop or two in cup of cold water. If it forms a soft ball in your fingers, add butter, baking powder and vanilla, and stir well.

Remove pan from fire. Cool until lukewarm, then beat until creamy and thick enough consistency to spread over cake.

Snow Caps

1¼ cups milk
4 oz (115 g) butter
6 oz (170 g) flour
4 eggs, separated
Vegetable oil for frying
Castor sugar
Powdered cinnamon

Boil the milk and butter. Stir in the flour and cook till the batter leaves the sides of pan. Remove pan from fire.

Beat into batter the 4 egg yolks and, when smooth, beat in the egg whites which have been whisked into a stiff froth.

Heat oil in deep pan. Drop in 1 teaspoon of the mixture at a time and fry till golden brown. Remove from pan, drain on paper, dredge with castor sugar and powdered cinnamon and serve.

Coconut Candy

3 cups grated coconut,
    pressed down slightly
3 level cups sugar
¼ cup evaporated milk
1 dessertspoon butter
Pinch of salt
1 teaspoon vanilla

Put all the ingredients except the vanilla in pan, stir well and cook over very slow fire until sugar is dissolved and mixture is boiling. Stir constantly with long wooden spoon to prevent burning. A stronger flame can be used after mixture boils, but use a smaller flame when mixture begins to thicken.

Cook until mixture is thick and forms a lump that leaves the sides of pan and begins to crystallise around the mouth of pan.

Add vanilla, stir well and place on buttered platter. Spread out with wooden spoon and knife but do not beat down. Let top have a rough surface. When slightly cool, cut into pieces, but do not separate pieces until candy has cooled sufficiently to be hard. Go through the grooves with a knife and separate into pieces.

Note:
If pink or green candy is required add as much cochineal or green colouring as you like, when candy is almost ready to be removed from the fire. If cocoa is to be added to give a chocolate flavour, add about 3 dessertspoons cocoa when mixture is boiling.

Serikaya

Malaysian Egg and Coconut Milk Steamed Custard

½ cup thick coconut milk
  from 1 coconut
10 eggs
1 lb (455 g) fine sugar
½ teaspoon vanilla essence

Remove dark skin of coconut before grating. Without adding water squeeze out thick milk from this through muslin.

Beat eggs gently with egg whisk without causing too much frothing. Now add the sugar and continue to beat, preferably by hand, to dissolve the sugar.

Add the coconut milk and vanilla and keep beating till sugar is dissolved. Pass mixture through thin muslin into an enamel container which has a cover. Steam for 3 hours till custard sets.

Notes:
This will keep several days if put in refrigerator.

Leave out vanilla if you like flavour of pandan. Run a fork through a leaf, make a knot of the strands and put it in the egg mixture when you begin steaming it. Remove leaf before custard sets.

Use container from tiffin carrier for steaming Serikaya.

Steamed Pulot & White Beans

2 cups pulot (glutinous rice),
  washed and drained
2 cups coconut milk from
  1 coconut, remove dark
  skin before grating
Salt to taste
½ cup boiled white beans
  (blackeye peas), the kind
  used in Lepat Kachang

Put pulot, coconut milk and salt in container from tiffin carrier. Cover and steam till pulot is half cooked. Stir in the beans and steam for another 15 minutes or till cooked.

Serve with fried Coconut Sambal (page 131).

Note:
This is an imitation of Lepat Kachang. It was a good and nourishing dish for breakfast or tea in the war years.

Easy-to-make Tapioca Cake

4 cups grated fresh tapioca
A few drops of cochineal
Grated coconut from
  ½ coconut mixed with
  ½ teaspoon table salt
1 cup thick gula melaka syrup

Half fill deep pan with water, bring it to the boil, turn down heat to allow water to boil slowly.

Divide grated tapioca into 8-10 portions. Colour some portions with a few drops of cochineal.

Make each into a compact ball in your hand, squeezing out a little of the liquid, then press into a circle ¾ in (about 2 cm) thick. Drop gently into the boiling water. Continue to do the same with the other portions.

When cooked the tapioca lumps will float. Remove with perforated spoon onto plate with grated coconut. Roll the lumps in coconut and put on platter. Serve with gula melaka syrup.

To make gula melaka syrup:
Boil ½ kati (10½ oz, 300 g) gula melaka pieces in about 1½ cups water till it thickens.

Strain through fine plastic sieve. Cool before using.

Steamed Tapioca Cake

2 cups grated fresh tapioca
1 cup water
A few drops of cochineal
Grated coconut from
  ½ coconut mixed with
  ½ teaspoon table salt
Thick gula melaka syrup
  (see above)

Mix the grated tapioca, water and cochineal. Put into a sandwich cake tin and steam for about half an hour or till cooked. Remove from pan and cool.

To serve, cut into pieces, roll in coconut and serve with gula melaka syrup.

Sweet Tapicoa Cake

Kueh Bengkah

5 cups grated fresh tapioca
1½ cups sugar
4 cups coconut milk from
   1½ coconut, remove brown
   skin before grating
1 level teaspoon salt
1½ oz (45 g) butter

Mix all ingredients, except butter, in a large basin.

Use some of butter to grease a large Pyrex dish or two small dishes.

Pour mixture in, put dabs of butter on top and bake in moderate oven for 1½ to 2 hours, or until pudding sets and has a golden brown crust on top.

Keep pudding overnight so that it can be cut into slices as hot tapioca pudding has a sticky consistency like glue.

Note:
Drain off some of the liquid if tapioca is very watery after grating.

Savory Tapioca Cake

For dried prawn preparation:
4 red chillies
8 small onions
3 oz (85 g) good dried prawns
2 dessertspoons oil
Salt to taste

For tapioca base:
5 cups grated fresh tapioca
4 cups coconut milk from
   1½ coconut, remove brown
   skin before grating
1 level teaspoon salt
1½ oz (45 g) butter

Pound chillies and onions till fine. Pound prawns till well broken up. Heat oil in pan. Fry onions and chillies, add prawns, and cook till fragrant. Keep aside.

Mix together all ingredients for the tapioca base, except butter, in a large basin.

Use some of butter to grease the large Pyrex dish or two small dishes you are using for baking the pudding.

Combine the tapioca base with the dried prawn preperation and salt to taste. Pour mixture into dish or dishes, put dabs of butter on top and bake in moderate oven for 1½ to 2 hours, or until pudding sets and has a golden brown crust on top.

Keep pudding overnight before cutting into slices as hot tapioca pudding has a sticky consistency.

Savory Tapioca Cake

Tapioca & Coconut Sugar Squares

1½ katies (2 lb, 900 g) fresh
  tapioca
1 cup thick gula melaka
  syrup (see page 255)
2 cups or more grated
  coconut, brown skin to be
  removed before grating
¾ teaspoon salt

Remove skin from tapioca. Cut into 3 in (7.5 cm) lengths and boil in water, to which a little salt has been added, till cooked. Drain away water, put pan on small flame to allow tapioca to get dry.

Place cooked tapioca on platter, remove centre fibre, mash with fork, adding the gula melaka syrup gradually according to your taste.

Do not mash tapioca too smoothly, but give the mixture a coarse texture. Place the sweetened mashed tapioca in a square or rectangular Pyrex dish and press down with fork to make it firm and compact. Put aside to cool, but not in the refrigerator.

Cut into small squares, roll in grated coconut to which a little salt has been added, and serve.

Sweet Potato Pudding

1½ cups boiled and mashed
  sweet potato
2 dessertspoons custard
  powder
4 dessertspoons sugar
½ teaspoon salt
2 eggs, beaten
1 cup of coconut milk from
  ¾ coconut, removing brown
  skin before grating
1½ oz (45 g) butter

Boil sweet potato in skin till well cooked. Remove skin, mash and cool, removing strings. Measure 1½ cups of this, place in a basin and mix well with all other ingredients except for butter.

Grease a pyrex dish with a little butter, pour mixture into it, put dabs of butter on top and bake for 1½ hours or till pudding sets. Cool and put in refrigerator. Slice and serve.

Sweet Potato Cakes

1 kati (21 oz, 600 g) sweet
  potato
1 dessertspoon cornflour
Salt
Oil for deep frying

Savoury Filling:
8 small onions
2-4 fresh red chillies
4 oz (115 g) dried prawns,
  cleaned and soaked in
  warm water and then
  drained
Salt to taste
3 dessertspoons oil

Sweet Coconut Filling:
2 cups grated coconut,
  removing brown skin
  before grating
1 cup gula melaka syrup
  (see page 255)

Boil the sweet potato and then mash, removing strings. Add the cornflour and salt and mix well, adding a little water to make the mixture hold together and not crack. Make compact balls of this, each as large as a walnut.

Take each ball, make a hole in the middle, fill with savoury or sweet filling. Close up hole securely, make ball compact again and place aside in plate. Fill all the balls in the same way.

Heat enough oil in pan for deep frying. Fry the balls till golden brown and serve.

Savoury filling:
Pound onions and chilllies to a smooth paste. Then add prawns and pound till well broken up. Add salt to taste. Heat oil in pan and fry pounded ingredients till fragrant, adding a little water to make filling moist enough to hold together.

Sweet Coconut filling:
Boil coconut and gula melaka syrup together till dry, stirring all the time.

Variations:
Instead of using mashed sweet potato for the balls you can use: 1/2 kati (10 oz, 300g) grated raw tapioca with 1/2 kati boiled and mashed sweet potato or grated raw tapioca alone.

Boiled Sweet Potato Balls
Ondeh Ondeh

3 cups cooked and mashed
  sweet potato
Cornflour, enough to form
  handable dough
Gula melaka, broken up
Grated coconut from
  ½ coconut, remove brown
  skin before grating
Salt

To the mashed sweet potato mix in cornflour to make a handable dough. Make balls with some gula melaka inside. Drop balls into slowly boiling water and cook till they rise to the surface.

Remove balls on to grated coconut, to which a little salt has been added. Roll the balls in coconut and serve.

Savory Pumpkin Cake

3 dessertspoons oil
2 dessertspoons sliced small
  onions
2 fresh chillies, finely sliced
6 dessertspoons dried
  prawns, cleaned, washed
  and pounded a little
Salt to taste
3 cups mashed boiled
  pumpkin, reserve water
1 cup rice flour

For topping:
Fried onions
Dried prawns, pounded and
  fried a little
Chopped celery
Sliced red and green chillies

Heat oil in pan, fry the onions, add chillies and dried prawns. Add 2 dessertspoons water and a little salt and cook till dry and fragrant.

Mix the fried ingredients with the mashed pumpkin and rice flour, adding some of the water in which the pumpkin has been boiled to make a moderately soft mixture. Add salt to taste. Put mixture in greased dish and steam for 1½ hours or till cake sets.

When cake is a little hard, sprinkle on the topping.

Continue streaming till cooked. Cool, cut into slices and serve. To improve taste, fry slices a little before serving.

Variation:
Instead of pumpkin, you can use boiled mashed yam. For this use only ½ cup rice flour.

Note:
This made a good breakfast dish during the war years when bread was not available.

Tapeh
Fermented Glutinous Rice

3 cups pulot (glutinous rice),
  washed and drained
2 cups water
2 level teaspoons ragi
  (locally made yeast)

Put pulot and water in a pan with a cover and steam till pulot is cooked but grainy. Spread cooked pulot on a platter to cool a little.

Pass the ragi through a fine wire sieve. Measure two level teaspoons of this and, when the pulot is just a little warm, sprinkle the powered ragi on it. Mix the pulot and ragi well.

Put into a glass bottle with a wide mouth. Put a circular piece of banana leaf on top of the pulot, cover the bottle and keep it in a box surrounded and covered with a few layers of cloth for 36 hours to ferment.

Chill tapeh before serving with or without sugar.

Variation:
For pulot hitam, add 2½ cups water for steaming.

Hoen Kwe with Grated Coconut & Gula Melaka

½ cup Hoen Kwe
  (green bean) flour
3 cups water mixed with
  ½ cup evaporated milk
3 dessertspoons sugar
A few drops of cochineal
1½ teaspoons instant coffee
Grated coconut from
  ½ coconut, remove brown
  skin before grating, mixed
  with a little salt
Thick gula melaka syrup
  (see page 255)

In a deep saucepan mix the Hoen Kwe flour, diluted milk and sugar properly before cooking it on a medium heat. Stir all the time, till mixture boils and has a shiny appearance.

Remove from heat. Divide mixture into three parts, leaving one part in the pan, and the other two in separate bowls. Mix a few drops of cochineal in one portion to get the pink you want. Add 1½ teaspoons instant coffee to another portion and leave the other portion white.

Using a dessertspoon fill small jelly moulds with the mixture and, when set, chill in refrigerator before serving. Turn the small coloured cakes on to a plate and serve with grated coconut and gula melaka syrup.

Cornflour & Gula Melaka Mould with Coconut Sauce

For the Cornflour Mould:
½ cup thick gula melaka syrup
4½ level tablespoons cornflour
2 cups water
1 egg white beaten to a stiff froth

For the Coconut Milk Sauce:
1½ teacups coconut from ¼ coconut, remove brown skin before grating coconut
½ teaspoon salt
1 dessertspoon cornflour

To make the gula melaka syrup, boil 2-3 oz, 55-85 g, gula melaka in ¼ cup water and strain.

For the Cornflour Mould:
Cook the gula mekala syrup, cornflour and water together, stirring all the time till mixture boils and thickens.

Cool a little and then fold in the egg white which has been beaten to a stiff froth. Put into a mould and chill in refrigerator. Serve with hot coconut milk sauce.

For the Coconut Milk Sauce:
Put all ingredients in a small pan and bring slowly to boil, stirring all the time.

Serve this sauce hot with chilled cornflour and gula melaka mould.

Soft Spongy Hoen Kwe

½ cup Hoen Kwe (green bean) flour
1 cup sugar, or to taste
3½ cups coconut milk from 1 coconut, remove dark skin before grating
½ teaspoon salt
A few drops of cochineal
1 egg white, beaten to a very stiff froth

Mix flour, sugar, coconut milk and salt together. Cook on slow fire, stirring all the time to prevent lumps forming, till mixture thickens and boils.

Remove pan from heat. Add a few drops of cochineal evenly or unevenly to suit your tatse. Then fold in, while mixture is still hot, one egg white beaten to a very stiff froth. Pour into mould.

Cool and put into refrigerator to harden before cutting into pieces with a brass fluted knife.

Three Layer Hoen Kwe & Coconut Milk Cake

½ cup Hoen Kwe
  (green bean) flour
1 cup sugar, or to taste
3½ cups coconut milk from 1
coconut, remove dark skin
  before grating
½ teaspoon salt
A few drops of cochineal
1½ dessertspoons cocoa

Mix flour, sugar, coconut milk and salt together. Divide into three equal portions and cook each separately on slow fire, stirring all the time to prevent lumps forming, till mixture thickens and boils.

Keep one portion white. Add a drop or two cochineal to one portion. Add 1½ dessertspoons cocoa and 1 teaspoon Hoen Kwe flour, which has been made into a smooth paste with 2 dessertspoons water, to third portion while it is boiling.

Pour chocolate portion into a square or rectangular Pyrex dish. After a few minutes pour over the chocolate layer the white portion and, after a few minutes, pour the pink mixture over the white.

Cool and put into refrigerator to harden before cutting into pieces with a brass fluted knife.

Notes:
If you wish to cook the whole quantity at once you can do so. When mixture is boiled, separate into three equal parts and colour each as you wish. Arrange layers as you like.

Brass fluted knives can be purchased in Chinese shops selling brass cooking pans, cake moulds, etc.

Variation:
For a change, place slices of steamed Pisang Rajah between the layers.

Sago Pudding

2 cups sago
2 egg whites
1½ coconuts
1 lb (455 g) gula melaka
¼ teaspoon salt

For the sago mould:
Clean the sago, wash it and after draining in colander, put it in deep pan of boiling water. Stir well and cook until sago becomes clear. Pour into a large wire sieve and let cold water from tap go through the sago, stirring it to get rid of the starch. Put sieve over large bowl to allow all water to drain away.

Beat egg whites to a stiff froth, adding a pinch of salt to it. Fold this into the sago in the wire sieve and then put sago into pudding moulds. Chill in refrigerator.

For the coconuts:
Remove the dark skin of coconut and grate it. Add to it about 3 teaspoons of cold water and ½ teaspoon salt and squeeze milk out through strainer into jug. Do not chill this.

As coconut milk becomes rancid very quickly this should be prepared from fresh coconut just before serving.

For the gula melaka:
Place the gula melaka which has been broken up a little in a pan, add 1½ cups water and boil on slow fire till sugar dissolves. Strain through fine sieve into a jug.

To serve:
Turn sago mould into dish, Serve with coconut milk and sugar which have been put in separate jugs. Amount and thickness of coconut milk depending on individual taste. Use more coconut if you want a richer pudding.

Note:
Good sago will not become starch during boiling.

Sago Pudding was sometimes called Singapore, Penang, Malacca Pudding, Straits Settlements Pudding, or Palm Pudding. Serve after a hot rice and curry lunch.

Papaya Jam

1½ lb (680 g) ripe papaya, grated
4 tablespoons lime juice
2 tablespoons grated fresh ginger
1 lb (455 g) sugar

Put all ingredients in porcelain dish, mix well and allow to stand for 6 hours. Then cook in enamel pan on slow fire for about 1½ hours or till jam thickens and sets when tested in a saucer.

Note:
Increase or reduce amount of lime juice and ginger to suit your taste.

Pineapple & Apple Jam

3 cups diced fresh pineapple
3 apples, removed skin and core and cut into pieces
2 cups sugar
A small stick of cinnamon

Put all ingredients in deep enamel pan and boil for about 1¼ hours, till jam reaches the right consistency. The pineapple will be in pieces but the apple will dissolve and thicken the jam.

Fruit Salad

2 cups coarsely diced ripe pineapple
2 sweet apples
2 pears
2 oranges
12 maraschino cherries, quartered
¾ cup sugar made into a syrup with ½ cup water, strained and cooled
1 dessertspoon lime juice, if desired

Skin and core apples, pears and oranges. Dice coarsely.

Mix all ingredients, chill and serve with whipped cream or ice cream.

Variation:
Add sliced bananas, if you like, just before serving.

Pineapple & Papaya Salad

2 cups coarsely diced ripe
  pineapple
4 tablespoons castor sugar,
  or to taste
4 cups coarsely diced ripe,
  but firm, papaya
2 dessertspoons limes juice,
  or to taste

Mix pineapple with sugar. Let it stand for 10 minutes. Then gently mix to papaya and lime juice, if required. Chill and serve.

Longan & Watermelon Salad

1 tin longans and/or
  1 tin lychees
6 cups watermelon balls

Mix the longans andor lychees, including the syrup, with the watermelon balls and chill.

Variation:
Substitute the watermelon balls with 4 cups of coarsely diced ripe pineapples.

Soursop Ice

1½ cups soursop juice from
  ripe soursop
1½ dessertspoons gelatine
3 tablespoons hot water
3 tablespoons sugar
2 eggs
1½ cup evaporated milk
2 tablespoons chopped
  maraschino cherries

Remove skin and seeds from ripe soursop, cut into pieces and press juice out by using a wire sieve.

Dissolve gelatine in hot water and add sugar, stirring till it dissolves.

In a bowl beat eggs with rotary beater, add the gelatine mixture, the soursop juice and milk. Beat well.

Pour into container and place in freezing chamber of refrigerator till it hardens. Cut into pieces and serve granised with chopped cherries.

Note:
Use apricot, peach or pear necter instead of soursop.

Ginger Syrup

½ lb (225 g) fresh ginger
6 cups water
5 cups sugar
1 egg white
1 egg shell
Red or green colouring

Remove skin from ginger, wash and grate. Add 6 cups water to the grated ginger and strain liquid into bowl through fine muslin. Let ginger powder settle at the bottom.

Pour out gently the ginger liquid, leaving behind the powdery part, to make 5 cups. Put this in an enamel pan with sugar. Bring to boil, stir till sugar dissolved and add the egg white and crushed egg shell. Boil slowly for about 40 minutes. Strain through fine muslin into porcelain bowl.

Add a few drops of green or red colouring. Bottle when cool. Serve with soda water and ice.

Limau Nipis Juice

6 cups coarse white sugar
3 cups water
1½ cups lime juice from
    local limes (limau nipis),
    seeds removed

Boil together the sugar and water and when sugar is dissolved strain through thin muslin. Put syrup in clean pan, add the lime juice and boil on slow fire for 20 to 30 minutes. Cool. Remove froth and bottle.

Notes:
Add more sugar if you like a very sweet juice. If you use limau kesturi (calamansi), which is less sour, use the same recipe, only reducing the water to 2 cups and sugar to 4½ cups.

Rose Syrup

3 cups sugar
2½ cups water
White and shell of half an egg
Cochineal
Rose essence

Put sugar and water in enamel pan and bring to boil slowly. When sugar is dissolved, add egg white and shell, crushing it a little. Let this simmer for half an hour to thicken and clarify syrup.

Pour through thin muslin into porcelain bowl. When cool, add a few drops of cochineal and a few drops of essence of rose.

Variation:
If you like pandan flavour, leave out essence of rose and add 2 shredded pandan leaves to boiling syrup.

Handy's Fruit Drink

2 cups stewed diced pineapple
2 cups freshly made lime
    juice from limau nipis
6 oranges, peeled, seeded
    and diced
¼ cup chopped maraschino
    cherries
6 glasses water
Crushed ice

Mix all ingredients in large bowl and serve in glasses with teaspoons, increasing or reducing water to suit taste.

For preparing the Stewed Diced Pineapple:
4 cups ripe pineapple, freshly diced
2 cups sugar

Boil pineapple and sugar for 15 minutes till sugar is dissolved. Place in porcelain bowl to cool. Use as required.

Almond Jelly with Lychee & Watermelon

1 cup loosely packed agar-agar which has been softened in cold water
2½ cups water
¼ cup sugar
¼ cup almond powder, mixed into a smooth paste with ½ cup cold water
½ cup undiluted evaporated milk
A few drops of green colouring, if desired
1 tin lychees, chilled
Watermelon, scooped into balls

Put the softened agar-agar strings in a cup to drain away the water. Put the agar-agar in pan with 2½ cups water. Boil this till agar-agar is dissolved.

Add sugar, almond paste and milk. Add food colouring if using. Stir till this boils. Pour mixture through fine plastic or metal strainer into jelly mould which has been rinsed with cold water. Allow jelly to set before putting it in refrigerator to cool.

To serve, unmould jelly into a large round dish, which is a little deep. Pour round the jelly a tin of chilled lychees or lychees mixed with small rounds of red watermelon.

Apricot Jelly

2 dessertspoons granulated gelatine
4 tablespoons boiling water
2½ tablespoons sugar
1½ cups apricot nectar
½ cup evaporated milk
1 egg white

Dissolve gelatine in boiling water. Add sugar and apricot nectar. Stir well and then add milk. Chill a little in refrigerator.

Beat egg white to a stiff froth, and pour over it the chilled mixture, beating the egg white into it. Put mixture into jelly mould and place into refrigerator to set. Serve with thin custard (see page 250).

Variation:
For variety, use peach, prune, loganberry or pear nectar. With Pear Nectar Jelly add chopped cherries and serve with orange custard.

Soursop Jelly

1 cup soursop juice from
   ripe soursop
5 tablespoons water
2 dessertspoons gelatine
2 tablespoons sugar
¾ cup evaporated milk
3 teaspoons chopped
   maraschino cherries
1 egg white, beaten to a
   stiff froth

For custard:
½ cup evaporated milk
½ cup water
3 dessertspoons sugar
1 teaspoon custard powder
A pinch of salt
¼ teaspoon vanilla essence

Remove skin and seeds from ripe soursop, cut into pieces and press juice out by using a wire sieve.

Boil the water, remove from fire and dissolve the gelatine and sugar in it. Then add soursop juice and evaporated milk. When jelly begins to set, add the chopped cherries and fold in the egg white. Pour mixture into jelly mould and chill in refrigerator. Serve with thin custard.

To make custard:
Mix all the ingredients except the vanilla essence in a small enamel pan, and bring to the boil, stirring all the time to keep custard smooth. When mixture boils add vanilla.

Serve either hot or cold with soursop jelly.

Agar-Agar Chocolate Pudding

½ cup agar-agar
1 cup water
¾ cup evaporated milk
   diluted with ¾ cup water
4 dessertspoons sugar
¼ teaspoon salt
2 dessertspoons cocoa
½ teaspoon vanilla
1 egg white, beaten to a
   stiff froth

Soak agar-agar in cold water, pressed down a little.

Boil agar-agar in water till dissolved. Add milk, sugar and salt. Mix cocoa with a little hot water to make a smooth paste, and stir into mixture.

Allow to simmer for five minutes. Pour through fine wire sieve into bowl. Add a few drops of vanilla and beat in egg white. Pour into mould, cool and then chill in refrigerator.

Serve with thin custard (see page 250).

Mango Fool

4 - 6 green mangoes, skinned and grated to the seed to give 1½ cups grated mangoes
3½ cups water
1¼ cups sugar
2½ cups evaporated milk

Boil grated green mango in ½ cup water, till it softened. Add sugar and the rest of the water. Add evaporated milk and set aside to cool.

Serve with grated ice, adding water and if necessary sugar, to suit your taste.

Notes:
This make a refreshing drink on a hot day. Green mangoes are usually available at Kandang Kerbau Market.

Agar-Agar Delight

1 cup agar-agar
2 cups water
¾ cup sugar
1 cup evaporated milk
A few drops of cochineal
Juice of 1 or 2 limes to make 1 dessertspoon, or to taste
1 egg white, beaten to a very stiff froth

Soak agar-agar in cold water, pressed down a little.

Boil agar-agar in 2 cups of water till it is all dissolved. Add sugar and when dissolved add in milk stirring till it boils. Remove pan from cooker, strain through fine wire sieve into porcelain bowl. Add a drop or two of cochineal and the lime juice that has been strained previously.

When jelly is cool and beginning to set fold in the stiffly beaten egg white and pour into the mould or moulds and chill in refrigerator.

Serve with thin custard (see page 250).

Agar-Agar, Gula Melaka, Coconut Milk Pudding

¾ cup thick gula melaka
   syrup
1 cup agar-agar
1½ cups water
¼ teaspoon salt
2 cups coconut milk from
   1 coconut, remove brown
   skin before grating

To make gula melaka syrup:
Place 5 oz (140 g) gula melaka in pan with 1 cup water. Boil till sugar dissolves and thickens a little. Strain before use.

To make pudding:
Soak agar-agar, loosely packed, in cold water to soften.

Put agar-agar in deep pan, add 1½ cups water and boil slowly till agar-agar is dissolved. Add ¾ cup gula melaka syrup and the salt.

When boiling add the coconut milk, and keep stirring till mixture begins to boil again. Remove from fire and pour through thin sieve into a square Pyrex or aluminium dish. Allow to cool before putting into the refrigerator. To serve, cut into pieces, choosing shape required.

Note:
If you want a hard jelly, use 1 cup of tightly packed softened agar-agar. When this jelly sets the coconut milk rises to the top, leaving a dark brown layer below.

Agar-Agar Drink

For jelly:
2 cups agar-agar, loosely
   packed
5 cups water
1 cup white sugar
A few drops of cochineal
   for colouring

For Rock Sugar Syrup:
1 kati (21 oz, 600 g) gula batu
   or rock sugar
3½ cups water
2 pandan leaves, through
   which a fork has been run
   lengthwise, tied into a
   bundle
White and shell of half an egg

To make jelly:
Soak agar-agar in cold water, pressed down a little, to soften.

Boil agar-agar in water till dissolved. Add sugar and when boiling add a few drops of cochineal to make a rather dark pink. Strain through fine sieve into Pyrex dish and allow to cool before chilling in refrigerator.

Just before serving cut jelly into pieces and scrape over coarse grater to make thin strings of pink jelly.

To make Rock Sugar Syrup:
Boil together sugar and water till sugar is dissolved. Put in the pandan leaves and egg white and the crushed shell to clarify syrup. When syrup is clear, strain through fine sieve into bowl.

Variation:
If you do not care for the pandan flavour use vanilla essence instead.

Serve in glasses, a little of jelly and syrup added in water and ice to suit your taste.

Chendol

1 cup Hoen Kwe
  (green pea) flour
1 lb (450 g) gula melaka
2 coconuts
Crushed ice
½ teaspoon salt
2 pandan leaves

For the flour preparation:

Mix in deep pan 1 cup of the flour and 4½ cup of cold water, breaking up the lumps. Cook over slow fire, stirring all the times to prevent lumps forming, till mixture thickens and boils. Remove from fire.

Place chendol frame over basin half filled with cold water. Place the cooked flour, a little at a time, on the frame and with a flat wooden spoon press the flour through the holes into the water. As the hot flour passes through the holes it will break and form little hard pear shaped lumps. Drain the water away and place the flour preparation in a bowl and chill in refrigerator.

Note:

If white Hoen Kwe is used, add cochineal or green colouring while cooking the mixture. If a large quantity is required, make one batch of each colour – green, red, white and mix them when serving.

For making the Gula Melaka Syrup:

Break up the sugar blocks into small pieces, add 2½ cups water and boil slowly on low fire till sugar dissolves. Add shredded pandan leaves for flavouring. Strain syrup through fine sieve into bowl.

For preparing the Coconut Milk:

Remove the brown skin of coconut before grating on fine grater. Add 2 teacups cold boiled water to make first squeeze, then add 2 teacups to make second squeeze. Add pinch of salt to each squeeze.

To serve, put 2 tablespoons of the Hoen Kwe preparation into small Chinese bowls, add syrup, crushed ice and coconut.

Snacks

Cheese Puffs

2 eggs
1 cup milk
1 cup flour
1 teaspoon baking powder
Pinch of salt and pepper
1 cup grated cheese
Oil for frying

Beat egg and add milk. Add flour which have been sifted with baking powder and seasoning. Beat well. Add cheese.

When thoroughly mixed, drop by spoonfuls into boiling hot oil. Fry till golden brown. Drain on brown paper and serve.

Cheese Straws

4 oz (115 g) flour
3 oz (85 g) butter
4 oz (115 g) grated cheese
1 egg yolk
A pinch of salt
A pinch of pepper

Put flour into dry basin, add butter and work in with finger tips. Add cheese, egg yolk, salt and pepper and mix together well.

Roll out and cut into straws. Bake in moderate oven for 20 minutes or till golden brown. Allow to cool before removing from pan.

Mrs P L Peach's Cheese Straws

½ cup flour
1 teaspoon baking powder
½ teaspoon salt
½ teaspoon paprika or chilli powder
1 tablespoon butter
1 cup soft breadcrumbs
2 tablespoons milk
1 cup grated cheese

Sift flour, baking powder, salt and paprika together. Rub in butter with finger tips. Add breadcrumbs, milk and cheese and mix thoroughly.

Roll to 6 mm thickness on floured board. Cut into narrow strips and bake in moderate oven for 20 minutes or until golden brown.

Cheese Toast

8 oz (225 g) grated cheese
1 egg
1 tablespoon melted butter
2 tablespoons milk
1 teaspoon mustard
Pepper and salt, if necessary
1 lb (450 g) bread cut into
    small slices (2 x ½ in,
    5 x 2.5 cm)
2 rashers of bacon,
    if required, cut into fine
    strips

Mix cheese, egg, butter, milk and seasoning well together, spread on bread, decorating top with strips of bacon.

Grill or bake in the oven until brown.

Fried Bread & Cheese Squares

4 tablespoons grated cheese
1 dessertspoon cornflour
1 beaten egg
2 tablespoons milk
½ teaspoon paprika or chilli
16-18 small squares of bread
Oil for frying

Mix all the ingredients except the bread and oil into smooth paste and put on bread quite generously.

Heat oil of ¾ in (2 cm) depth, and when hot fry bread squares, cheese side first. When cheese becomes golden brown, turn over.

When bread is golden brown, remove, drain on paper and serve hot.

Prawns on Toast

1 lb (455 g) prawns, shelled,
cleaned and chopped very
    finely
1 dessertspoon finely
chopped celery
2 beaten eggs
1 tablespoon cornflour
Salt and pepper to taste
24 small thin squares of
    bread
Oil for frying

Mix the prawns, celery, eggs, cornflour, salt and pepper well. Spread on bread squares quite generously.

Heat oil in frying pan to depth ¾ in (2 cm). When hot, fry bread, prawns side first. When prawn becomes golden brown, turn over. When bread is golden remove, drain on paper and serve hot with mustard.

Note:
If you like the flavour of onions, add to mixture 1 dessertspoon diced onions, fried first in a little butter.

Minced Meat & Bread Squares

2 dessertspoons butter
½ large onion, finely diced
½ lb (225 g) minced beef, veal
  or lean pork
Salt and pepper to taste
2 potatoes, boiled and
  mashed
2 eggs
1 dessertspoon chopped
  celery and spring onion
Thin slices of bread cut into
  1 x 2 in (2½ x 5cm) pieces
Vegetable oil

Heat butter in pan. Fry onions till slightly brown. Add minced meat, then salt and pepper to taste. Fry till well cooked.

Mix the above, when cool, with mashed potato, 2 beaten eggs, chopped celery and spring onion leaves, and more salt and pepper to taste.

Put the mashed meat and potato on the small thin pieces of bread.

Fry in deep oil. Drain on paper and serve with freshly made mustard, tomato sauce or chilli sauce.

Note:
To save oil, heat ½ in (about 1 cm) of oil in frying pan. Fry bread squares, meat side first. When golden brown, turn and fry till bread is golden brown on other side.

Bhajias
Savoury Gram Flour Fritters

½ lb (2 cups, 250 g) besan
  (gram flour)
2 tablespoons diced onions
4 green chillies, sliced finely
1 teaspoon baking powder
1 egg, optional
Salt to taste
About 2 cups water
Vegetable oil for frying

Mix all ingredients, except oil, into a thick batter by adding as much water as is necessary. Drop a teaspoonful at a time into hot deep oil. Drain on paper and serve hot.

For variety:
Slices of large onion, brinjal, pieces of cauliflower and spinach leaves dipped into this batter and fried makes a pleasant change.

Note:
Gram flour, called besan, can be obtained along Serangoon Road from Indian shops that sell curry spices.

Austrian Fritters

½ teaspoon baking powder
3 tablespoons icing sugar
1 teaspoon powdered
  cinnamon
A pinch of salt
¼ pint (140 ml, ⅔ cup) water
1½ oz (45 g) butter
2½ oz (70 g) flour
2 eggs
Vegetable oil for frying
More icing sugar and
  cinnamon for coating
  fritters

Mix together the baking powder, icing sugar, cinnamon and salt.

Place water, butter and salt in pan and boil. Add in all the flour. Stir till well mixed and mixture leaves sides of pan and forms a ball. Take off fire. Cool.

Add eggs, one at a time. Beat till light, adding the baking powder etc. Shape into small balls, using two spoons, and fry balls in deep fat till they brown. Balls should swell to a little more than twice their size.

Drain on brown paper, and when cool, roll in icing sugar and cinnamon and serve.

Fried Potato Balls with Curry Filling

4 oz (115 g) plain flour
3 oz (85 g) butter or
   margarine
4 oz (115 g) boiled potato,
   mashed
2 dessertspoons water,
   for binding
Salt and pepper to taste
Curried minced beef, pork
   or chicken or Savoury
   Filling (see below)
Vegetable oil for frying

With fingers rub fat into flour to form consistency of breadcrumbs. Add the mashed potato, binding with water and seasoning with salt and pepper.

Make into balls, flatten out, fill with minced curry, close the balls and fry in enough hot oil to cover balls in a small kwali or pan till all golden brown.

Drain on absorbent paper and serve.

For variety:
Instead of boiled potato you can use boiled yam.

Savory Sandwich Filling

1 chicken breast
1½ dessertspoons butter
1 dessertspoon flour
¼ cup chicken stock
2 dessertspoons tinned
   cooked ham, diced
2 dessertspoons tinned
   mushrooms, diced
2 dessertspoons tinned red
   pimentos, diced
2 dessertspoons tinned or
   frozen green peas
¼ cup evaporated milk
Salt and pepper to taste

Steam breast of chicken with salt and pepper, remove skin and dice. Keep stock.

Melt butter in frying pan, add flour. Blend to a smooth paste, adding the chicken stock gradually. Add all other ingredients and the evaporated milk, and salt and pepper to taste.

Note:
If you use frozen peas, boil before using.

For variety:
Make choux pastry shells using the recipe on page 234 and fill with any savoury sandwich filling or any minced meat and curried meat.

Curry Sandwich Filling

1 cup of minced cold beef,
   chicken or mutton curry
2 dessertspoons curry gravy
Salt if necessary

Mix all ingredients and spread on buttered slices of bread.

Savory Buns

For filling:
1 lb (455 g) lean pork or beef
  or chicken breasts
Pinch of salt for meat
Pinch of pepper for meat
½ teaspoon thick soy sauce
1 level dessertspoon coriander
1 small piece cinnamon
½ teaspoon peppercorn
3 dessertspoons butter or
  vegetable oil
4 small onions, finely ground
2 medium-sized potatoes,
  diced
1 dessertspoon finely diced
  black dried mushroom
1 dessertspoon finely diced
  preserved sweet marrow
  rind (tungguah)
Salt and sugar to taste

For yeast mixture:
1 cup flour, sifted
1 oz (30 g) yeast
1 oz (30 g) sugar
1 cup warm diluted
  evaporated milk

For buns:
1¼ lb (570 g) sifted flour
Extra flour for kneading
1 teaspoon salt
2 oz (55 g) sugar
3 eggs yolks, beaten
2 oz (55 g) melted butter
2 eggs whites, whisked to a
  stiff froth
½ cup warm diluted
  evaporated milk

To make savoury filling:
Rub a pinch of salt, pepper and soy sauce over the meat you are using. Put a dessertspoon butter in pan, fry the meat a little on both sides, add ½ cup water and cook till meat is done. When cool, cut into pieces and pass through mincer. Put aside till required. Grind coriander, cinnamon and peppercorns together.

Put 2 dessertspoons butter in pan. Fry the ground onions till golden brown. Add the ground spices, fry a little, then add the diced potato and a little water. Cover pan. When potato is soft, add all other ingredients, mixing thoroughly and adding salt and a little sugar to taste. When mixture is just moist remove from pan on to a plate. Cool before using.

To make yeast:
Mix the yeast mixture ingredients into a smooth paste in a deep enamel cup. Leave in a warm place to rise.

To make buns:
Pour flour in enamel basin, make well in the centre, add yeast mixture, sugar, salt, two beaten egg yolks and melted butter. With a wooden spoon stir flour gradually into mixture and beat till smooth. Beat the whisked egg white and continue beating till bubbles begins to form.

Cover basin with cloth and set aside in warm place to rise. When dough has doubled its bulk, put dough on floured wooden board and knead, adding enough flour to make a handable dough.

Cut it into sections, roll each on a floured board and cut into pieces (1½ in, about 4 cm, square). Roll each into a ball, press into circular shape, put 2 teaspoons of savoury filling in centre, and draw edges together. Place on buttered baking sheets, closed end down.

Leave buns to rise to double their bulk. Brush tops with milk and remaining yolk, which have been beaten together, and bake in hot oven for 30-40 minutes.

Vegetable Curry Rolls

Filling:
1 cup potato cubes
1 cup cauliflower cubes
1 cup carrot cubes
1 cup frozen peas
2 level dessertspoons butter
  or margarine
1 large onion, diced coarsely
2 level dessertspoons curry
  powder, mixed into a paste
  with 4 dessertspoons water
½ cup water
Salt to taste

Pastry:
4 oz (115 g) butter or
  margarine
¼ teaspoon salt
4 oz (115 g) self-raising flour
  and 5 oz (140 g) ordinary
  flour, sieved together into a
  basin
About ⅓ cup iced water
1 egg, beaten

For making filling:
Potatoes, cauliflower and carrots should be of ½ inch (about 1 cm) cubes.

Heat butter in pan, fry onions till soft, and add curry powder paste. Fry for two minutes and then add all vegetables, water and salt. Cover pan and cook on moderate heat till vegetables are cooked and a little moist. Remove to plate to cool.

With a fork, mash the potato slightly so that the vegetables will stick together a little.

For making pastry:
With a fork, mix the butter and salt into the flour till you have the consistency of breadcrumbs. Add the iced water, a little at a time, mixing lightly with finger tips till a soft rollable dough is formed. Cut into four equal pieces.

For making curry puffs:
Flour a wooden board and rolling pin. Shape one lump of dough to make a rectangular shape, and roll it out to make a 8 x 5 in (20 x 12 cm) rectangle of ¼ in (about ½ cm) thick.

Put some of the curry mixture along the middle of length of the rectangle. Now place one end of the dough over the curry. Brush beaten egg on other end and place it over the first.

Turn over the long roll on the board, and with a sharp knife cut the roll into 5 or 6 pieces. Place pieces in a greased baking sheet. Repeat the process to use up the dough and curry.

Brush tops of these vegetable curry rolls with beaten egg and bake in oven (400°F, 200°C) for 40 minutes or till rolls are golden brown.

Fried Potato Curry Puffs

Filling:
½ kati (10½ oz, 300 g) lean
  pork or beef, boiled and
  minced
2 dessertspoons oil
1 large onion, diced
2 rounded dessertspoons
  curry powder made into
  paste with water
Salt to taste
2 medium sized potatoes,
  boiled in jackets, skinned
  and diced
A little coconut milk or milk
Green chillies, sliced, optional

Pastry:
2 cups flour
½ teaspoon baking powder
Salt to taste
4 rounded dessertspoons
  margarine or butter
1 egg, beaten a little
Cold water, enough to make
  soft dough
Oil for frying

For making filling:
Place oil in deep pan, fry onions till golden brown, add curry paste, stirring for a few seconds.

Add the meat, mix well, fry for about ten minutes. Add salt, cover pan and cook till meat is tender.

Add potatoes, green chillies if using, and coconut milk. Cook till potatoes are done and the filling is dry.

After filling is cooked, place it in a dish tilted on one side to allow oil to drain away from meat. Cool before using.

For making pastry:
Sift flour, baking powder and salt into basin. Add margarine and work lightly into flour with fingers until mixture has texture of fine crumbs. Add beaten egg. Add water to make soft dough and knead for a few minutes.

For making curry puffs:
Break off ½ the dough and roll out on floured board to thickness of ⅙ inch (4 mm). Cut into rounds with a small glass and remove rounds to floured plate. Roll each round to required size and thickness.

Fill each round with filling, press edges and flute edges or press edges with fork.

Fry in hot vegetable fat till well done, turning when necessary. Drain on brown paper and serve.

Note:
Sliced green chillies can be added to curry after it is cooked to make the filling hotter.

Sambal Goreng Sandwich Filling

½ kati (10½ oz, 300 g) fresh
 prawns
2 dessertspoons vegetable oil

Ground very finely:
1 stalk of serai (lemongrass),
 sliced
2 thin slices lengkuas
 (galangal)
3 buah keras (candlenut)
6 chillies, seeded
½ teacup small onions

Salt to taste
½ teacup coconut milk from
½ coconut
Lettuce or sliced cucumber
 if desired

Shell, clean and steam the prawns. When cool, keep
the prawn juice aside. Mince the prawns.

Put oil in pan, and when hot fry ground ingredients
till well cooked. Add minced prawn, stir, add prawn
juice, salt and coconut milk. Cook until the Sambal
Goreng filling is a little moist.

When cool use for sandwich filling with lettuce or
sliced cucumber.

Sardine Sandwich Filling

1 small tin sardlines
Yolks of 2 hard boiled eggs
Salt, pepper, mustard,
 vinegar or lime juice to
 taste
2 dessertspoons melted butter

Remove bones and dark skin from sardline, mash to
paste, add egg yolks, salt, pepper, mustard, vinegar
and melted buttered. Mash together till smooth.

Spread mixture between slices of buttered bread,
adding thin slices of cucumber.

Chicken Sandwich Filling

1 cup minced cold chicken
 left over from a roast or
 stew
3-4 dessertspoons salad
 cream
Melted butter or rich chicken
 stock or gravy to moisten
Salt and pepper to taste

Mix together all ingredients and use for sandwiches.

For variety:
2 dessertspoons minced ham in place of the chicken
added to ingredients above makes another good
filling.

Egg & Cheese Sandwich Filling

2 eggs
2 tablespoon evaporated milk
Pinch of salt
Pepper to taste
1 dessertspoon butter
1 oz (30 g) cheese
1 tomato, cut into very thin
  slices, if desired

Beat eggs, add milk, salt and pepper. Put butter in pan and pour in mixture, cook over slow fire, stirring all the time, till it thickens and becomes creamy. Transfer to plate and mix cheese into mixture till smooth.

Spread on buttered slices of bread to make sandwiches. Use slices of tomato, if you like, between slices.

Salmon Sandwich Filling

1 small tin salmon
4-6 dessertspoons salad
  cream or 3 dessertspoons
  salad cream and
  2 dessertspoons sandwich
  relish
Pepper and salt, if necessary
Lettuce, if desired

Remove bones and dark skin from salmon, mash, adding salad cream and relish and pepper and salt.

Spread on thinly sliced and buttered bread, using lettuce leaves between slices.

Index

Page numbers in bold indicate dishes which are illustrated.